TRINITY

ALSO BY JOSEPH F. GIRZONE

Joshua

Joshua and the Children

Joshua in the Holy Land

Kara, the Lonely Falcon

The Shepherd

Never Alone

Joshua and the City

What Is God?

Joey

A Portrait of Jesus

Joshua the Homecoming

Jesus His Life and Teachings

The Parables of Joshua

JOSEPH F. GIRZONE

TRINITY

IMAGE BOOKS

DOUBLEDAY

NEW YORK   LONDON   TORONTO

SYDNEY   AUCKLAND

IMAGE

AN IMAGE BOOK
PUBLISHED BY DOUBLEDAY
a division of Random House, Inc.
1745 Broadway, New York, New York 10019

IMAGE, DOUBLEDAY, and the portrayal of a deer drinking from a stream are
registered trademarks of Doubleday, a division of Random House, Inc.

Trinity was originally published in hardcover by Doubleday,
a division of Random House, Inc., in 2002.

This Image Books edition published by special arrangement with Doubleday.

Book design by Jennifer Ann Daddio

The Library of Congress has cataloged the Doubleday hardcover edition as follows:

Girzone, Joseph F.
Trinity / by Joseph F. Girzone.
p. cm.
1. Trinity. I. Title

BT111.3 .G47 2002
231′.044—dc21
2002019298

ISBN 0-385-50458-6

March 2004

First Image Books Edition

1 3 5 7 9 10 8 6 4 2

INTRODUCTION

I address this book to those who already believe in God, as they would be the most likely persons interested in a deeper understanding of God. The Trinity is not a theological definition. It is the very nature of God. It is the God we worship. God revealed himself to us through Jesus, not so he could be imprisoned in a theological concept to be memorized as a condition for baptism. He revealed himself to us because he loves us and wanted to share himself, his inner self with us, so we could come to know and love him as he is. We have received that revelation with cruel indifference, wondering why God even bothered to reveal something that we could hardly understand. But rare faithful souls who take Jesus' words to heart and draw near to God in the intimacy of contemplative prayer eventually experience the ecstatic joy of being embraced within this inner life of God. They know, from their own inner revelation, this Triune God whom the rest of us can only try to define. Indeed, we would do much better to imitate them, in welcoming the Trinity into our hearts rather than struggling to define it.

There are, however, those who say they do not believe. By this they often mean that they do not believe in the God so many believers profess, because although they profess to believe, they do not act as if they believe, and mirror in their ungodly lives a god who is dysfunctional and merely a mimic of capricious human emotions and responses. So, it may be that even those who profess not to believe may find comfort and enlightenment in reading the following pages, with the hope that they may find an image of a God who is believable, and perhaps, even lovable.

Christians, Jews, and Muslims believe in the one, same God. They may use different names, but it is clear that the essence behind the names is that of the God we all believe in and worship. We believe that God is the only God. Essential to the nature of God is infinity, without limits, so logically there can be only one who is without limits in being and in power.

When it says in sacred scripture that man is made in the image and likeness of God, it is important to understand what that means. Not properly understanding its meaning can cloud our idea of God, for it is only too easy to place on God the limits of our humanity. God then becomes a mirror image of our humanity, with the same limitations and change in moods common to humans. That is a fatal mistake that causes so much confusion in our attempts to understand God. We then look upon God as human like ourselves, and assume that he reacts to us and the things we do in the way we might react to one another. It is one of the reasons we are prone to fear God, because humans express anger in often hurtful ways when we are displeased; so God must be the same when we displease him.

Even though we say God is all-compassionate, deep down we do not believe it. We may say it in our prayers, but we rarely take it seriously enough to apply it to life. We are too prone to view God in his justice as vengeful and punishing. Indeed, some people *delight* in the idea of a punishing God who will one day avenge the hurtful deeds done to them by their enemies.

If we are to have at least a faint glimmer of the essence of God's being and magnificence, it is critical that we erase the preconceived human images of God that have been nurtured in various ways throughout our lives. God is as far above us as the stars are above the earth. He is too great and too wonderful and too unfathomable to be squeezed into a human form and made to conform to our image and likeness.

The only way we can ever come to know God is if he condescends to tell us about himself. In the following pages we hope God will guide us to a deeper understanding of himself and his compassionate love for those whom he has been pleased to give life and to offer eternal life in his presence.

TRINITY

One

GOD THE CREATOR

It was the second day of Christmas, and, even though his coming warmed our hearts, it was very cold outside. The fire in the fireplace I built not only for atmosphere but to warm the chill inside. Sitting before the fire, I soon became mesmerized by the darting flames burning brilliantly, though soon the intense heat forced me to move farther back for comfort. Staring at the flames, I noticed how they not only warmed the room but cast their luminous spell all across the foyer.

I was immediately reminded of God. There was the fire, and the light that comes from the fire, casting its mystic glow throughout the room, and the warmth that comes from the fire through the flames, warming every object around it. Yet the flames were not the fire, nor was the heat the flames. The three were distinct, but they were inseparable, save for how they each affected me. The light and the heat touched me immediately. The source of the fire was present but could not be seen.

My memory wandered back many years, to one evening when I was baby-sitting my lawyer's children, Joe, John, and Peter. Richard and Elizabeth Della Ratta had asked me to mind the boys until they returned. At bedtime, as I tucked in the little ones, Peter said to me, "Fahd, I have a problem with God."

"Pete, you're only six years old. How can you have a problem with God?"

"But, I do, Fahd."

"How come you only have problems when you're going to bed?"

"It's the only time I have to talk to you."

"Okay, Pete, what's this big problem you have with God?"

"Fahd, when you tell me about God, you talk about God as our Father, and you talk about Jesus, and you also talk about . . . the . . . you know, the other guy."

"The Holy Spirit."

"That's right. Now, you talk about these three people, and you tell me there is only one God. If there are three of them, how can there be only *one* God?"

"Pete, God is not like us humans. God's nature is different. See that lamp there? There is the bulb, there is the light coming from the bulb, and there is heat coming through the light from the bulb. They are all different, but you can't separate them. They're all together as one. That is something like what God is like."

"But, Fahd, God doesn't work on electricity."

"Pete, why don't you just close your eyes and think about it? I'm sure it will put you right to sleep."

As I went back downstairs I thought, "How young we are when we begin to question about God. We humans are born philosophers, with a thirst to understand our existence. I suppose once we experience the vastness of the world and all the complicated beings in it, it is only a simple next step to ask ourselves where it all came from, and who made it, and then the whole train of questions that logically follow.

Now as I sit before the fire in my study, my mind wanders back to Moses and his experience with the burning bush, the bush that burned but was not consumed. I am sure the voice he heard that day haunted him all his life.

"Moses, come no closer! Take off your shoes, for the ground on which you stand is holy ground! I am the God of your fathers, the God of Abraham, the God of Isaac, and the God of Jacob."

God then goes on to tell Moses that he is concerned about his people in Egypt, and how they are sorely hurting from the cruelty of their slave drivers. Interesting. I sometimes have a problem with how so many people view the Bible as inspired. I have no doubt that God's inspiration guided each author to write, but as to what God intended people should accept as inspired is perplexing. Some say each word is inspired. Others who are familiar with the history and literary forms of the Bible's books have a more open understanding of inspiration. That something happened to Moses on Mount Horeb that day, when he saw the burning bush and heard the voice of God, I have no doubt. What is so thought provoking about that incident is that Yahweh showed concern for his people suffering so harshly in Egypt. That speaks volumes. The idea alone of God communicating with a creature is stunning. But the age old question "Does God really care?" is answered in that scene. A new facet of God. And if one can readily accept as historically true that Moses did experience the presence of God that day, and if one can be convinced of

God's concern for his human creatures, that can form a solid basis for one's concept of God. That God does care for us I have never doubted, in spite of all the confusing, tragic events that take place in our lives. However, it is difficult for many to believe, or be convinced: that God really cares. This was brought across to me rather dramatically one evening in Switzerland.

Seven years ago, our dear friends, Bill and Anna Belle Bru, invited Sister Dorothy and me to Switzerland to speak to a group of their friends. When we arrived at their château, we were surprised that half of the group of 150 people were atheists or agnostics. The night before the talk, we were invited to a formal dinner at the home of one of their friends. There were a number of important people there, among them Jan Martensen, the Swedish ambassador to Switzerland. He had also been the Undersecretary General of the United Nations. Jan was a delightful individual, and we parted feeling very close to each other, though it did not start out that way.

As we were sitting down to dinner, Jan was the last to take his seat. As he sat down, he made the remark, out of nowhere, "I can't understand why anybody would worship a God who allows all the evil in the world to take place."

Sister Dorothy was sitting way down at the other end

of the long table. She signaled me to keep my cool and say nothing. But I knew Jan was expecting me to react, from a brief exchange we had a few minutes earlier.

No sooner had Jan got the words out, than everyone's eyes went down toward their soup. No one wanted to get involved in that issue. Everyone sensed that statement was directed to me. At first I said nothing. Then Jan continued. "I have an even more difficult time understanding why anybody would dedicate their whole life to a God like that."

Well, I knew Jan was not being nasty. He was genuinely grappling with a problem that had tortured him all his life, and no one was interested in his question or able to give him a believable answer, and I felt he was merely throwing out the issue for someone to come up with an answer that made at least some sense.

I said, "Jan, the problem you have, and others like you, is that you really don't believe that free will is a good thing."

"What do you mean by that?"

"Very simply. God must have thought a long time before he finally decided to give his human creatures freedom to make their own decisions. Once he did that, he was stuck with all our nonsense and abuse of freedom. *You,* and others like you, would have God continually interfere in human decisions to prevent people from doing evil, so we could have an evil-free world. God, fortunately, has more respect for our freedom than that."

That response, however, did not sway Jan. "Why is there so much injustice and hunger and poverty in the world, and so much suffering?" he continued.

"Jan, why do people have to blame God for that? Suppose you were a multibillionaire and while traveling on safari you came across a group of people in a forsaken place. They were poor, hungry, ravaged by disease. You felt sorry for them, but knowing you could not stay there, you picked a few highly intelligent and educated persons among them and gave them directions on how to save their community. You made arrangements to give them hundreds of millions of dollars to accomplish the task. Then you left.

"After your departure, the persons you entrusted with the task thought to themselves 'Why should we waste all this money on those people? They are only rabble anyway. With this money we are wealthy beyond our dreams. Let us keep the money for ourselves,' which is what they did.

"When the rest of the community saw what had happened, could they blame the kind rich man for not helping and healing them?"

Jan agreed it would not be reasonable to place the blame on him.

"That is what God is like. He has blessed us with resources far beyond what the world needs, so that we could care for one another. Is it right to blame God for the greed and selfishness of those who have so much and refuse to share? And if the world's diplomats could get their own hearts in the right place, they could do much to bring the rich and the powerful together to solve the problem of starvation and injustice."

Even that did not deter Jan. The frightful issue had haunted him for too much of his life to lose this chance to possibly find an answer.

After letting him speak for a while, I said, "Jan, you amaze me."

"What do you mean?"

"I am a priest. I write books. Yes, I believe in God. I pray in my own simple and inadequate way, and I try to say nice things about God in my writings, but I sense that I spend nowhere near the time thinking about God that you do, this God in whom you say you do not believe. Jan, I do admire you. And I am sincere in saying that. Most people, when they come across the idea of evil in the world, are so overwhelmed by the thought, they put it out of their minds and refuse to think about it ever again. But you have hung in there all these years, and are still struggling to understand God. You're a rare human being, Jan. I admire you for it."

"Father, I like you," he said with a broad grin. "I came to the dinner tonight so I wouldn't have to go to your talk tomorrow, but I'll be there."

With that matter settled, the dinner was delightful and we all had a most enjoyable time. The rest of the guests even enjoyed the unexpected entertainment.

After dinner Jan took me aside and said, "Father, I have been to so many formal state dinners, often with the diplomatic corps and Vatican officials. I have to tell you, the Vatican diplomats are brilliant. You can tell they are the only ones who are professionally trained for their work. But in all the years I worked with them, not one of them ever talked to me about God."

I could feel his painful disappointment.

The next day, after the talks that Sister Dorothy and I gave about Jesus, I hadn't noticed Jan until I walked through the crowd. A man grabbed my arm. I looked down. It was Jan. He had tears in his eyes. What a beautiful, peaceful smile he had on his face. All he said was, "Thank you, Father. Thank you so much." Then he worked his way through the crowd to find Sister Dorothy to say good-bye. I was deeply moved by the depth and honest goodness in that man. I would have liked to have had him as a friend. I regret that we have not kept in touch.

To me, Jan was a symbol of modern man and woman, cultured and highly intelligent, searching for a god in whom they can place reasonable belief, not a bourgeois god made to man's image and likeness, with all the faults, limitations, and prejudices common to humans, but the God who made sense to a person who was searching with an honest mind. And there is nothing wrong with that searching, for even Saint Peter encouraged the early Christians to "find a reason for your faith." Nor is it meant that God has to make "sense" in our worldly meaning of the word. God will never make sense in that way, for God's ways are far beyond the ability of the human mind to ever begin to understand. It is therefore impossible to find God through reason alone. Faith is first of all a gift. God may reward our search for him and allow us to find him at the end of our search, but it is not our search that found him. It is his gift at the end of our search that opens our hearts to embrace him, though not everyone receives this gift. And even though many may spend their whole lives searching for him and not find him, that does not mean that they are alienated from God. God is aware of their painful search. God has need of those people to witness to him in other ways. They are still doing his special work in their lives, though they may never realize it. They are close to God as long as they never give up the search. For them, their search is credited to them as faith as Abraham's obedience was credited to him as faith, and as such will be ultimately rewarded.

One summer after my ordination, I took some courses at Columbia University. One day my physics professor and I were on the elevator together. He remarked to me, "Father, I envy you Catholics. You are such a happy lot. I see all the other students crowding around you after class, wanting to spend time with you. Most of them are Jewish, like myself, and they seem to have so much fun when they are with you. I was born and raised in South Africa. I went to a Jesuit university and studied Catholic philosophy and theology, hoping that I could find faith, but it has always eluded me. I prayed so hard for faith, but I never found it. Why can't I believe? How does one get faith?"

I looked at him and felt sadness in my heart for the anguish that pained him so deeply. All I could say was, "I guess faith must be a gift, but God rewards our searching."

Unfortunately, the elevator reached our floor and after we parted, our relationship went back to that of professor and student. I guess the privacy of the elevator was something like the confessional, where deeply private thoughts can be shared and painful burdens momentarily shed. I would have liked to have had a chance to share with him and have allowed him to share with me each of his experiences, as I would have shared mine as well. Sometimes it can be a great comfort just to share. It can give us insights into the various and mysterious ways God works through each of us, while loving us all with remarkable tenderness.

Two

GOD THE PROVIDER

Tenderness. That is another trait manifested in God's revelation of himself to Moses, and through history, as recorded in the Hebrew scriptures. The story of Adam and Eve, though it may be a poetic way of describing the origins of humanity, shows a God who is incredibly condescending in his love for these new creatures he has just brought forth. He has placed them in a veritable paradise and suspended the laws governing his creation to provide a comfortable environment for this special couple. He spends special intimate time with them each evening. He has even shared his own life with them, which they were to pass on to their children if they remained faithful.

One thing, however, God could not do: He could not force them to love him. Love is the free choice of the will reaching out to embrace something beautiful that the intelligence sees as good. By its nature, love has to be free. For that, Adam and Eve had to make their own choice. When they were given that choice, they decided that to be independent and live as they desired was at that point a more attractive good than humble dependence on God. They chose to walk their own way through life. In doing that they gave up not only those special gifts for themselves, but lost them for their children and their descendants forever. That is what is meant by original sin: being born with all the natural gifts due to human beings, but without those special gifts that were beyond what was natural. Among those was that special gift of intimacy with God. Even though God could no longer allow them to live in their cozy paradise, he still sent them off with promises of love, protection, and of a savior who would one day win back for them and their descendants the gifts that they had thrown away. A strange God, indeed, when you consider the idea of gods that people worshiped at the time the Bible was written.

If the story is true that Moses and the Israelites spent forty years wandering through the wilderness (and there is no reason to doubt the historical accuracy of the important events of those years), that again portrays a most unusual God. Those hundreds of thousands of people had to be fed miraculously during all those years. There was no food in the desert to satisfy the needs of that many people. The guidance and protection and comfort God gave his people during that time is also remarkable. The world has never known a god of such benevolence and care for his creatures.

In later years of Israel's growth in the Promised Land, God continued to show kindness toward his people, through miraculous interventions on numerous occasions, and his protection in difficult times. Though scripture writers may have interpreted adverse historical events as harsh punishments from God, it does not seem when analyzing these events, whether they be epidemics or military conquests by Israel's enemies, that they manifest God being vindictive or capricious in his treatment of Israel. It is more the people's own actions that resulted in consequences that were inevitable, and painful.

In establishing a priesthood for Israel, God assured that the priests would provide guidance for his people, especially with respect to their continuous instruction in his law. This priesthood and their assistants, the scribes, were the teaching authority, or the official magisterium, of the religion God set up for them. As long as the priests and scribes remained loyal to God, they were also faithful in communicating God's wishes to his people. However, at times when the teaching authority slipped away from its responsibility and did not reflect the will of God for his people, God then bypassed the religious authorities and used prophets to deliver messages directly to the people. Here is where God shows his concern and love in most remarkable ways, not only by continual warnings of inevitable consequences of the people's infidelity, but by touching expressions of his "pain" over their ingratitude and unfaithfulness. God even compares himself to a bridegroom, and Israel to his dearly beloved bride who has broken his heart by her continual infidelities. "I remember the affection of your youth, the love of your bridal days. You followed me through the wilderness, through a land unsown. Israel was sacred to Yahweh, the first fruits of his harvest. . . . What shortcomings did your fathers find in me that led them to desert me? . . . They never asked, 'Where is Yahweh, who brought us out of the land of Egypt, and brought us through the wilderness.' " (Jer. 2, var. verses) What god ever spoke to creatures in that way in all of human history?

We can easily see that we are witnessing a most extraordinary manifestation of divinity. And it is not myth. It is history. To this point God manifests himself as the beginning and source of all existence. He is Yahweh, whose essence is existence itself. He is unique and one and there is no other like him. He has no equal nor any other even similar. He is exceptional in his Oneness. This idea was branded into the consciousness of the Israelites. This Oneness of God was never to be challenged or even doubted. To impress this upon the people's consciousness, Moses forbade the construction of any temple other than the one which God ordered as his home. As there is one God, he lives in only one place. When the temple was constructed in Jerusalem, that was the place where God dwelt. There was never to be any other, lest people begin to wonder whether there might be another god. Throughout Israel, gathering places were constructed to facilitate community prayer and worship services and where scriptures could be studied and expounded. They were just that: community gathering places called "synagogues."

Though God tried hard to show love for the people, and to draw them into his tenderness, they never seemed to understand, and forever drifted from his care and concern. When evil befell them, they were inclined to blame their problems on God for not taking care of them. In time they became more frightened of him than trustful. Their image of him remained rigid and unchanging, though he tried so often to soften their understanding of his relationship with them. They seemed never really to understand him or his spirituality, or the spiritual nature of his dreams for them, and drifted into more worldly fantasies.

Even though the Jewish people's predominant idea of God was his Oneness, there is a stunning incident in Genesis in which God seems to have hinted at the unique nature of that Oneness. One day, as Abraham was sitting at the entrance of his tent near the oak of Mamre, three men approached. In these three men, Abraham saw Yahweh, and went out to greet him. Did Abraham see God revealed in a different way? Did he see God as a trinity? He sees three persons, but talks to them as if they are only one. He saw in those three men the divine Presence. He begged him to stay and spend some time with him, and told Sarah to prepare some food. Before the three men left, they promised that by the same time next year, Sarah would give birth to a son.

Even though the episode is difficult to interpret, the message is thought provoking, and seems to be, "When thinking of God, do not close your minds to a deeper understanding of what God may be like in reality. What you think him to be is not what God really is." Whatever the intention of God in that incident was, the hint is clear that God might not be like what people think he is like. He is much different in reality. That is the only mention in the Hebrew scriptures that God's nature might be different from what people thought.

In the Book of Wisdom, however, God reveals hints of his inner life and of his creative genius. The hints are almost humorous, as if God is teasing us to dare try to understand him. Those verses that are descriptive of God are so tantalizingly brief and enigmatic that they leave the reader suspended in total frustration. God, could you not have revealed more of yourself? What are you afraid of, God? There are some of us who crave to know more about you. Are we so hurtful and cruel that you are afraid to reveal yourself to us? Can you be hurt by your creatures? Yes, you were hurt, deeply hurt, when you revealed so much of yourself to the Israelites and they were unfaithful to you. And we are no better, Lord. In some ways, you are so much like us. Yet, you are so far from our humanness in the greatness of your goodness. You show none of the meanness and vindictiveness of our humanity, yet you can still be hurt by our insensitivity to your love. Although I cannot understand how God can be hurt, which seems to indicate that you are vulnerable, I must believe what you say, so I accept that you are in some way that I cannot understand, hurt by our indifference to your love and caring for us.

The Book of Wisdom continues its description of wisdom. "Within her is a spirit intelligence, holy, unique, manifold, subtle, active, incisive, unsullied, lucid, invulnerable, benevolent, sharp, irresistible, beneficent, loving to humans, steadfast, dependable, unperturbed, almighty, all surveying, penetrating all intelligent, pure, and most subtle spirits; for wisdom is quicker to move than any motion. She is so pure, she pervades and permeates all things.

"She is a breath of the power of God, pure emanation of the glory of the Almighty; hence nothing impure can find a way into her. She is a reflection of the eternal light, untarnished mirror of God's active power, image of his goodness. Although alone she can do all things, herself unchanging, she makes all things new. In each generation she passes into holy souls, she makes them friends of God and prophets; for God loves only the person who lives with wisdom. She is indeed more splendid than the sun, she outshines all constellations; compared with light, she takes first place, for light must yield to night, but over wisdom evil can never triumph. She deploys her strength from one end of the earth to the other, ordering all things for good."

Is this a descriptive definition of God? Is wisdom a facet of God? As God has no gender, is God revealing a facet of his being that bears traits humans consider feminine? Is it some revelation of God's being as akin to a marriage relationship? It is called an emanation of God's glory, giving perhaps a hint of an aspect of God unfamiliar to the Hebrew mind, distinct from the essence of the divine being, but inseparable from it. Such a description, written long before Jesus came to earth, would have been considered nothing more than a poetic description of God's own wisdom as it governs the course of creation, particularly that of God's human creatures. For people after Jesus' time, it would be clearly a hint of the uniqueness of God's being as having various facets of his essence, this one being the Holy Spirit, the creative facet of God.

Three

GOD EVER-PRESENT

The God of the Hebrew scriptures was a lovable, but almost lonely God, who craved the love of his creatures, whom he had chosen to be his own, though they rejected him time and time again. Reading carefully of God's involvement with the Jewish people, a very clear image emerges of a God who is not at all different from the God whom Jesus described for those willing to listen to him. He is a God who is amazingly like Jesus in his relationship with people.

Jesus never judged people by what was apparent on the surface of their lives. He saw what was in their hearts. His Father was the same. He chose a man like Moses, who, in a moment of anger had killed an Egyptian soldier who was beating an Israelite slave. God chose this Moses to confront Pharaoh and lead his people out of Egypt. Besides having killed someone, Moses was married to a pagan woman. These things did not seem to bother God. Once having settled his people in the Promised Land, his intimacy with his people is touching. He commands a Sabbath rest, not because he is concerned about his own worship services, but to protect slaves and the common people from being worked to death, and to provide the people with a day each week to enjoy their family's and their friends' companionship. Throughout the Bible, God issues laws and commandments, not to restrict people's freedom but because he wants people to care for one another and be honorable in their dealings with one another. His interest was intensely personal. He did not issue laws to make people's lives difficult. His love and concern for the downtrodden and the outcasts transcended the rigidity of Moses' laws. He could overlook the morally shabby lives of poor people, prostitutes, and other outcasts because his heart melted at the sight of their anguish and pain and loneliness. You see this on different occasions, even in the ones he chose as the ancestors of his Son. It was from the descendants of Rahab, the kind prostitute, who aided Joshua on his entrance into the Promised Land, that Yahweh would one day send his Son. It was also centuries later, through Solomon and the other descendants of Bathsheba, the former wife of Uriah, whom David had killed, that Jesus would be born, rather than from the descendants of David's first wife, who was honestly married to him. God could be strict and severe in ordering that the people keep his commandments, and punish them particularly for their injustices to one another, and for their meanness and cruelty, especially toward the defenseless. But his mercy and compassion was extraordinary when even the worst of sinners repented of their evil ways. As evil as David was at times, the sincerity of his repentance touched God's heart so deeply that God could still refer to him as a "man after my own heart."

Although God set up the priesthood and the scribes as the official teachers of the religion, he seems never to have had much respect for them, and often bypassed them, choosing prophets from among the people to bring his most important messages to the community. Jeremiah was the only prophet who was from a priestly family, but, when chosen, he had not yet entered into the politics of the religion and still maintained his youthful innocence. Most of the prophets the priests had killed, because they resented the prophets and their messages. Later, Jesus will accuse the scribes and Pharisees of being the descendants of those who killed the prophets, and of doing the same thing in their own time. "Your fathers killed the prophets, and you build their tombs."

Jeremiah's relationship between God and the people lasted a long time and was always tumultuous. His messages were rejected, and the inevitable consequences resulted. Not that God was punishing the king and the priests, but God foresaw the political consequences of their opposing the powerful king of Persia. Someone might ask, "Why did God put up with such obstinate resistance to his messages? Why did he not just leave them to their own devices?" Again, the answer seems to be always the same. He was in love with his people and no matter how obstinate and unfaithful they were, he would never abandon them, as he had so many times promised.

It is no different from Jesus' story about the prodigal son, which is really the story of the prodigal father. The prodigal father gives his son his part of the inheritance even before he dies. The son wastes it all on loose living. Then, falling on hard times, he decides to go back home, knowing his father will receive him with open arms, which is just what the prodigal father does. "Bring him in," he tells the servants, "clean him up, put a robe on him, put a ring on his finger, sandals on his feet. And kill the fatted calf, so we can celebrate." Jesus is intentionally showing how far his Father goes to show his love for all of us. The God whom Jesus reveals has not changed in all those centuries. He is still that unbelievably forbearing God who takes such abuse from his creatures yet never gives up in his endless attempts to win their love. It is hard to imagine a God so humbling himself for his creatures.

When you filter out the incidents in the Hebrew Bible in which evil events are attributed to God's anger with his people, and concentrate on the words of Yahweh, the same image of God emerges as the image that Jesus tried with such persistence to instill in the hearts of the people of his day, though without much success. It seems as if we have an innate resistance to accept as true the overwhelmingly tender and incomprehensible love that God has for us. There seems to be something in our nature that demands that God be an avenger of evil, a just judge demanding that all wrongs be set straight. It seems that only persons who have, with profound anguish, experienced the frailty of their own humanity, can appreciate a compassionate and forgiving God. And that is precisely the God who emerges from the lips of God himself in his utterances to the prophets.

The ancient Hebrews did look upon God with awe, and would never dare call him "Father." They were afraid even to use his name. They had the recorded memories of their ancestors who were with Moses as they crossed the desert, and had experienced the thunder and lightning and other awe-inspiring manifestations of Yahweh's might and grandeur on Sinai. This awe at God's majesty is reflected in the prayers in the Hebrew Bible. They are formal and carefully measured. Even David's psalms, as expressive as they are of the whole gamut of human emotions, and as much as David loves the Lord, his prayers are those of a loyal servant to a powerful king, a king who rewards those who keep his law. David's argument on his own behalf, in an attempt to convince God to show him mercy and to protect him from his enemies is that he is a faithful observer of the divine laws, precepts, and decrees. It is a kind God who shows mercy toward David, his faithful servant. Though David sings warmly of his love for God, there is that profound chasm that keeps him at a respectful distance from his divine Lord, like a soldier from a general he reveres. His prayer does not indicate that David looked upon God as a dear friend and warm companion; much less that he would ever call him "Abba," "Daddy," as Jesus was to teach his disciples to do. That would be too intimate. Indeed, a rabbi once told me that the idea of calling God "Father" is shocking to the Jewish mind. The awesome majesty of God is the image that the Jewish people understand and revere. It was for Jesus to forever change his Father's image in people's minds.

Four

GOD THE SON

Hail Mary, full of grace! The Lord is with you. Blessed are you among women! . . . You are to conceive and bear a son. You will name him Jesus. He will be great and will be called the Son of the Most High." These are the words of the archangel Gabriel announcing his message from God.

"How can this be, since I am a virgin?"

"The Holy Spirit will come upon you, and the power of the Most High will cast his shadow over you, and the child will be holy and will be called 'Son of God.' "

Who is this Holy Spirit? No one ever heard of a "Holy Spirit" before. In all the pages of scripture, the Holy

Spirit is never mentioned, except for the hint that is made in Genesis in the three men who visited Abraham, and in whom he saw God. The archangel Gabriel talks of the Holy Spirit as a person; and then talks of the Son of God, being brought to earth by the power of the Holy Spirit. These words come from the lips of an angel. And shortly afterward, when Mary visits her cousin Elizabeth, the elderly cousin, under the inspiration of the Holy Spirit, exclaims, "Who am I that the mother of my Lord should come to visit me?" The living person of the Lord is already present in his mother's womb, "Emmanu-el," God living among his people, even though only still an embryo.

More is revealed about the inner life of God in those two scenes than in all the rest of scripture. Who is this Holy Spirit? Is it just an expression of the power of God? But in the next phrase the angel then says "the power of the Most High will cast his shadow over you," so the Holy Spirit must be distinct from the power of God.

Certainly Mary could not have invented the name "Holy Spirit." She is the one who had to tell the story of how her Son came to be. How would something like that even cross the human mind, much less the mind of a young and innocent woman? And to even think of calling the child to be born "Son of God"? She was certainly not familiar with such things in Greek or Roman mythology. Mary was a first. She had no precedent that could even suggest an idea or phrase like that to her. The Gospel writers certainly did not know of such things to be able to attribute what happened to the action of the Holy Spirit. The wording itself is too original. And one thing the Gospel writers were not was original. They were faithful witnesses to what they had seen and heard, but original? No, and far from it. Thankfully.

And this use of the term "Son of God." Special people in the Hebrew Bible were called "sons of God," but now the term is used to define the nature of the child who was conceived without human intercourse and solely of the Holy Spirit, overshadowed by the power of the Most High. This is a stunning change in the image of the Almighty, an image no one is prepared to accept, much less understand. After being conditioned for thousands of years to think of God as one, now God himself redefines that image. He is one, but he is also three. Elizabeth may have, when filled with the Holy Spirit, referred to Mary as the "mother of my Lord," when she said, "Who am I that the mother of my Lord should come to visit me?" but what did she mean by that? Although she uttered those words under God's inspiration, did she realize fully what she was saying? Was she referring to Mary's son as "the son of David," a messianic title for the great King to come, or did God give her a deeper understanding of the mystery that was unfolding in both her own and Mary's lives, so that she knew this was the promised "Emmanu-el," the true Son of God? There seems to be a hint of that in the inspired words that follow. These two special women had a premonition that they were part of a mystery that was just beginning to unfold in the drama of Israel's destiny, and indeed in the destiny of humanity itself. And as God usually worked, he chose these two simple, faithful women, one carrying the last prophet of the Old Testament, and the other bearing the Son of the Most High, for whom that prophet would spend his whole short life, and in the end die for him.

This is the beginning of a drama, as the life of God himself is about to unfold on the pages of the Gospels. The circumstances surrounding Jesus' life as recounted in the Gospels are just the stories about the surface of his life. Those events were world-shaking in themselves, but the other drama was the one contained in what Jesus revealed about himself and his Father and the Holy Spirit. These are stunning revelations of the nature and inner life of

God, never before revealed, which caught the Jewish people totally by surprise.

The Jews had always looked upon God as awe-
inspiring and far above humans, but they had no way of
imagining what he would look like. Like the Romans and
Greeks, they probably imagined him to have some kind of
human form, although they were strictly forbidden by
Moses to craft any graven images of God or any other beings. The one thing that had been burned into their consciousness was that God was one. They had no reason to
think any farther. When Jesus came and began to tell the
people what God was really like, they were unprepared for
it, and it was too much for them to handle. It was obvious,
however, that it was important to Jesus that he reveal the
true identity of God. It was important to God the Father
that people know more about him. In fact, that became
the key drama in Jesus' mission. On practically every page
of the Gospels, Jesus mentions something about his Father, and then about the Holy Spirit. This insistence on
God as three, though still one, was not only confusing to
the Jewish mind, it bordered on blasphemy; it also was the
one issue which kept getting Jesus into trouble, and which
the Sanhedrin finally seized upon to condemn him for
blasphemy.

Interestingly enough, it was John the baptizer, not Jesus, who first mentioned the Holy Spirit, when talking to the crowds following him. "I baptize you with water, but there is one coming after me, someone more powerful than I, whose sandal straps I am not even worthy to unloose. He will baptize you with the Holy Spirit and fire." Where did John hear of the Holy Spirit? On the occasion of Jesus' baptism by John, Luke describes the incident as follows: "Now when all the people had been baptized and while Jesus, after his own baptism, was at prayer, heaven opened and the Holy Spirit descended on him in bodily shape, like a dove. And a voice came from heaven, 'You are my beloved Son, my favor rests on you.' "

Then almost immediately afterward, the Gospel says that "Jesus was led by the Spirit out into the wilderness." Isaiah talks of the spirit of the Lord, but it does not seem to be in the same sense as used by Jesus and the Gospel writers. This introduction of the Holy Spirit as a way of referring to God is such a dramatically new concept that it is difficult not to realize that God himself is introducing us to an aspect of his being that is important for his Son to share with us. He knew it would be confusing to the people and the religious teachers. It is not a concept that a human being would invent, especially a

Jew for whom the concept had no clear precedent. From a purely human point of view, it would have no purpose, or practical significance. But to God it was important that people understand this facet of his being, his essential nature. It was important enough to him that he would allow his Son to be continually harassed over this revelation, and the revelation of Jesus as the Father's only begotten Son.

On an occasion when the subject of Jesus' miracles came up for discussion, the Pharisees attributed Jesus' miraculous power to Satan. After countering their accusation, and asserting that his power was from the Holy Spirit, he threw a frightening threat back at them. "I tell you, everyone of men's sins and blasphemies will be forgiven, but blasphemy against the Spirit will not be forgiven. Anyone who speaks against the Son of Man will be forgiven, but if anyone speaks against the Holy Spirit, he will not be forgiven, either in this world or in the next." The reason being if Jesus is their Savior and the Holy Spirit is what inspires Jesus, by judging them both as evil, they would never look to them for forgiveness or for salvation and eternal life.

But now that the Holy Spirit has introduced us to Jesus, the Father's Beloved Son, understanding this Beloved Son becomes an urgency. What is this Beloved Son? Is he just a "son of God" like to all the other prophets and saintly souls graced by God's favor? No. He is the Father's *Beloved* Son, born of the Father's own essence. The Image of the Father in human flesh. As the Image born of the Father, he possesses all that the Father is, and as such he reflects in his own being the Father whose image he is. As Jesus himself is to say later to Phillip, "Phillip, have you been with me all this time and you still do not know me? Do you not know that he who knows me knows the Father also, because the Father and I are one?" If that is so, then one cannot help but wonder what the Jewish people saw when this Jesus came walking down the street. Was it a man of great dignity, radiating an aura of the awe-inspiring majesty of God? Hardly. Was he carefully dressed to reflect his innate nobility? Hardly. He had most probably slept up in the hills the night before, so his appearance would not make a very striking impression. He apparently presented a rather earthy image of a common ordinary working man. Was he a man rich in the things of this world? Certainly not. Was he well dressed? Not at all. His robe was, I am sure, not neatly pressed or spotless, but soiled from sleeping on the bare ground, as was often his custom. Did he carry a comb in his pocket to groom himself on the way down to the village? That is hard to imagine. But when most people looked at him, those things did not matter. There was something much more compelling about his demeanor. His gentleness, the look in his eyes, the love that radiated from his presence, revealed a person of extraordinary charm and charisma, which immediately drew people to him, as unassuming love can disarm and melt the hardest of hearts, and the most cynical of souls.

They saw a man rather lean and slightly tall, with a casual walk and ease of movement, but totally aware of everything around him. As eyes mirror the soul, in his look people saw a hint of the beauty and greatness of soul that was veiled by a humble, self-effacing demeanor. His glance passed through the facade of people's lives and saw into the frightening depths of their fears and insecurity. "You judge by what you see on the surface of people's lives," he once said, "but I judge by what I see in their hearts." When people looked into his eyes, they knew he was looking into their souls. But for some reason, that look was not frightening, nor was it critical or judgmental. It showed understanding and compassion. Though the ordinary people knew he was a good man, they also saw that his goodness was unlike the "holiness" of the scribes and Pharisees who, in their self-righteous arrogance, were only too ready to pass judgment on these crusty, unwashed elements of society. These very poorest of people were drawn to Jesus and he to them. He cared for them and was genuinely concerned about them. They saw in him a kind spirit, reaching out for their friendship. He knew who they were and what they were like. Many had no friends or were loathed by "nice" society. They liked this Jesus, and at the same time wondered what he saw in them that he should desire their friendship. The "nice" people, those obsessed with their own importance, on the other hand, stayed aloof and were wary and contemptuous of the unassuming simplicity of this wandering stranger.

He was not like other people. This was immediately obvious. He walked with an air of freedom, as if he had everything under control. Nothing frightened him. The pompous show of power and control on the part of the religious leaders and even the Roman military as they paraded through the streets made little impression on him. They were no different than the peacocks or roosters in the barnyard showing off their plumage. To him they would have been more ridiculous than frightening, had it not been for their meanness and injustice toward the poor and unprotected. Even nature, with all its unpredictable violence, like the storms on the sea, aroused not fear but wonder and awe at the power and beauty of his Father's creation.

Still, as noble as he was, he had none of the trappings of the great ones of this world that would hint that he was anything other than a simple peasant. Even though he could say to Phillip "When you see me, you see the Father," how could one expect the common people to see the Almighty and ineffable God in this unkempt man walking down the back streets through the bazaar full of hawkers and money changers? All they could see was that he was a calm man who walked calmly through life as if he were in complete control of not only his destiny but of everything around him. Calm, serene peacefulness was his signature. Those near him felt secure in that serenity.

As to his eating habits, it seemed he ate little; only what little he could pick up along the way as he traveled from village to village telling the people about his Father in heaven, the Yahweh they called their Lord and God. When people invited him to dinner, he rarely turned them down. In fact, it did not take long before he gained the reputation among the Pharisees for enjoying parties and good wine. On long journeys, however, when there were miles of nothing but barren land, he would go hungry, and that seemed to be often, as he was forever moving from place to place, so absorbed was he in his Father's mission that he was unaware of his own needs. On at least one occasion his family was notified that he had been preaching all day long and had not had a thing to eat. His mother and his kinsfolk were so worried they went out looking for him.

Five

THE WORD OF GOD
BECOMES MAN

What is this Word of God? A word is a thought or idea expressed. Saint John in his Gospel calls Jesus "the Word." He is the Thought or Idea of God expressed. God is, in his very essence, in his being, intelligent love existing, totally self-subsisting. He needs nothing and no one to fulfill his being. He contains all existence within himself. As intelligent love, God thinks and loves. His mind, in the beginning, produces only one Image, as there is nothing outside himself to consider. That one Image or Idea is perfect understanding of all that he is, containing in it all that there is in God, sharing even his existence. Since this is so, that Image must also be God, though distinct, yet inseparable, from the Mind that gives it life. Once that Image is born, endless creative possibilities arise, as all things created are created through that divine Image. Saint John expressed it in this way: "All things were created through him, and without him was made nothing that has been made."

Now we see two facets of God's being: God thinking, and the effect of that thinking, his Image. Did one precede and exist before the other? In humans that would be true, as the person must precede and exist before he can think, but in God it is not that way. God's nature is not as complicated as ours. God is perfect in his simplicity. The eternal Mind of God thinking existed simultaneously with the Image that was being born. There was never a moment in which God's mind was still. There was never a moment when the Image did not exist. The Image was of God's essence itself, something totally unique to God, as God himself is a totally unique being. That Image cannot be separated from God, but is a distinct person, though in all things identical to the Mind producing it, of the same substance as the Father, as theologians would say, while having its own identity as a person. Theologians have called it the Second Person in God. It is also called God's Son, his Only Begotten Son. Long before this Second Person came to earth in Jesus, he existed with his Father as they worked together in the happy adventure of forming in their common Mind all the living and nonliving objects they were to create.

When the Father decided to create, the Son was there with him. When the angels and the pure intelligent beings were fashioned and created, it was through the Son that they came into being, together with the glorious Kingdom of God's presence where they would enjoy life in the intimacy of his love forever. When space was created, it was through the Son that it came into being. When the primordial substance of the universe was designed, and primitive life was created with its still-unfolding myriad of evermore complex living beings, it was again through the Son that this genetic masterpiece came into being and began to unfold. When the Father decided to make man and woman in his own likeness, it was through the Son that these beings, humans with angelic souls, also was accomplished, with exquisite care and extraordinary love. At the moment God created space and matter, time also came into being, not as an entity in itself, but as the measurement of relationships between things and events already past with those present and those still to come, as they all relate to one another in the awareness of human consciousness. For with God there is no time, no past, no future, as everything is present in his understanding.

When we say that the Father created through the Son, is it the Father or the Son who creates? Perhaps the more precise way to express it is that the Son creates by the power of the Father. When the sun shines on a garden, it is not the sun itself that causes the plants to grow. It is the light from the sun shedding its rays on the plants that gives them life. But the light could not do that if it did not first radiate from the sun. So the sun causes the plants to grow through its radiance, which bathes the plants with its light. So when the Father creates, he creates through his life-giving energy which flows through his Son. "All that I have," Jesus said, "I received from my Father. The Father and I are One." So, although they both work together, it is proper to say that each Person performs his function in a distinct way, but not independently, or separately, from the others. For humans, this is difficult to understand, as we have no experience in life around us of the perfect simplicity of the divine nature. The functioning of their relationships is completely atypical. That is why it is so difficult to understand what God is like and how God thinks. We continually try to comprehend him in terms of what we know of human beings, particularly male human beings, and, in the process, lose ourselves in an intellectual labyrinth.

Six

THE HOLY SPIRIT

Other than the veiled hint in Genesis, we were introduced to the Holy Spirit by the archangel Gabriel in the Annunciation, when he told Mary that she would bear a child by the overshadowing of the Holy Spirit. Other events involving the Holy Spirit followed in rapid succession, clearly manifesting God's intent to reveal a much more profound insight into his identity than ever before.

After Jesus' baptism by John, the Synoptic Gospels relate that Jesus was driven by the Spirit into the desert to spend the time in prayer and fasting for forty days. That desert, a godforsaken chain of rocky cliffs, far down into

the valley lying between Jerusalem and Jericho, is a perfect, if frightening, site to spend time in deep thought and
prayer, far from the noise and distractions of human con-
course. It was along this lonely road, which winds down
the steep descent from Jerusalem to the ancient city of
Jericho, that the Samaritan would find the battered trav-
eler, lying there half dead. From his rocky retreat Jesus
could look across the valley and see history-rich Jericho
hidden among the date palms abundantly fed by Jordan's
pure waters as they spilled into the thick, brackish soup
called the Dead Sea, some nine hundred feet below sea
level, the lowest spot on earth.

"Driven by the Spirit," St. Mark's Gospel reads. Jesus
was not alone on retreat. It was a time of preparation for
the beginning of a ministry that would forever change the
destiny of humanity. It was a time to sift and sort. As
God's Son, Jesus knew his destiny. As Mary's son, he had
to learn things for the first time. Sorting and understanding the two sources of knowledge could be confusing. The
Holy Spirit's intimate presence would provide not only
light and understanding but comfort in that desolate
wilderness, as Jesus' human mind struggled to understand
what his divine mind already knew.

This is the first time we see the Son of God and the

Spirit of God in relationship. What was their relationship? Jesus always speaks with such affection when he talks of the Holy Spirit. What were they to each other?

We saw how the Mind of God gave birth to an Image that became an identical, living reflection of himself. But God also has a will, the ability to love. That is why we say, "God is Love." That, together with his intelligence, is also of God's essence. The Son, as the perfect Image of the Father, containing within himself all that there is in the Father, shares his Mind and his Will, the very essence of what constitutes divinity.

Not long ago, we had the great joy of helping a well-known Chinese Communist official, whom we had befriended, come to the United States and receive political asylum. At one point, while visiting with us, she revealed at breakfast that God had come to her during the night. "It was like a dream," she said, "but it was not a dream. God really came to me. God is so beautiful. God is all love." Tears then began to well up in her eyes, and she changed the subject. For a lifelong Communist, who had no idea of God, to say something like that is hardly imaginable, especially as there was no way in China to read or learn anything about God. To experience that God is beautiful and all love is something that we as Christians spend a lifetime trying to understand and be convinced of. To learn it in the flash of a moment is awesome, and a pure gift of God. What that woman experienced was the Spirit of God, the Holy Spirit, the love that proceeds from the Father and the Son. In that brief moment, she was overcome by the ineffable Spirit of God's love; indeed, a rare mystical experience for a Communist, and a person who had previously known nothing of God, having been torn from him as a child and kept isolated from him all her life.

This love which that woman experienced transformed her life. When she returned to China after her first brief stay here, the effect this transformation had on the 250,000 students in her charge was profound, and as a UNESCO official declared, clearly miraculous. During her final year as director of education, she instilled what she had learned into the hearts of her students, and during that year there was not one incident of crime or drug abuse throughout her whole vast school system, which spanned kindergarten to university level. Previously, drug abuse and crime were rampant. The power of the love that she herself had experienced, she was able to pass on to all those young people. It is a powerful manifestation of Jesus' words: "I have come to set fire upon the earth, and what more could I desire but that it be enkindled?" Love itself is what God is. It is the very heart of divinity, the cause of every living being in this world and in any other that may exist, and capable of transforming all that it touches.

This revelation of God to individual souls is not unique, nor is it rare. God has called us all to this intimacy, but few of us dispose ourselves to accept it. Jesus said on one occasion, "When someone accepts me, my Father and I come and live within that person." It is that simple. He is there to befriend us, to establish a relationship with us, to become our companion, our partner through life. This mystical relationship with God is capable of unlimited growth and development.

A beautiful example of how the Holy Spirit works in a human took place in the life of Saint Mary Magdalen dei Pazzi, a Carmelite nun born into a noble family. Each day as the nuns spent their hours in contemplation, she was carried away in ecstasy, and experienced the presence of God as Three Persons together as One. It was during those very difficult times in the Church when even the saintliest of people were often suspected of heresy. When the nun told her confessor what she had experienced, he could not believe that such a revelation was possible. He told her to write down all that she had experienced. As simple as the experience was for her, it took a whole volume to explain.

When she finished and handed it over to her confessor, he passed it on to a team of theologians, who, after reading it, were in awe at the theological accuracy of everything that that simple nun had related of her experience, things that many clergy could not even understand.

Jesus mentions the Holy Spirit frequently, and almost always as he enlightens the minds of the Apostles, or fills the hearts of his followers with wisdom and grace and spiritual gifts. As long as he was on earth with the Apostles, he taught them and guided them. But he promised that once he left, he would send the Holy Spirit to bring back to their minds all that he had taught them. It was his way of ensuring the integrity of his message until the end of time. If acceptance of his teachings was required of those who followed him, he had to ensure the faithful transmission of those teachings until the end of time. That was to be the role of the Holy Spirit: to mold the mind of the Church through each generation, so it could be a beacon in the spiritual darkness of people's ever-changing fashions in religious doctrines and morals.

The Holy Spirit played a critical role in Jesus' life while he was on earth. Whatever he did, he did under the prompting of the Spirit. Filled with the Holy Spirit, he was driven into the desert to spend his first forty-day retreat as he prepared for his ministry. Even as an infant being brought to the temple for his circumcision, the Holy Spirit prepared for his arrival. The old priest Simeon had been promised by the Holy Spirit that he would not see death until he had first seen the Messiah. He recognized the fulfillment of that promise when Jesus was presented to him for his dedication to God.

On other occasions, when Jesus prayed, he prayed under the inspiration of the Holy Spirit, as when he spontaneously burst into praise to his Father for having revealed to simple people truths he kept hidden from the learned and the clever. It was a comfort to Jesus, because the learned and the clever held him in low esteem while the children, young and old, opened their hearts to embrace him. They were a joy to him.

The Spirit was ever with him, being the bond of love between himself and his Father. Indeed, his Father was ever with him as well, since there was no separation between them. Each was forever present with the other, while they were at the same time individuals, and as such, distinct, though inseparable. Each shared the same thoughts, the same love, and the same dreams in their common intelligence and common will.

So we can see that God has to exist as a Trinity of

Persons: coeternal, never one existing before the others; co-extensive in all things, sharing equally their omnipotent mastery of all creation; knowing all things; loving without condition all that they have brought into being, forever loving and caring for all that they have made, especially those whom they fashioned like themselves.

It is now left to us to try to understand how the Trinity works in the world, and especially in the Church, as the extension of Jesus' presence in history, and also, how they work within us as we struggle along the pathways of life on earth.

Seven

"RECEIVE THE HOLY SPIRIT . . ."

After Jesus' resurrection, the Apostles were happy beyond description to see him alive again. The night of the resurrection, Jesus passed through the solid wall of the room where they were staying, scaring them out of their senses. Walking over to them, he said, "Be at peace. As the Father has sent me I also send you. When he had said this, he breathed upon them and said to them, "Receive the Holy Spirit; whose sins you shall forgive, they are forgiven them; whose sins you shall retain they are retained." Jesus had given them the Holy Spirit, but the meaning of those words were lost on them at the time. They just felt a peaceful serenity, knowing that he was with them again. Years later, when they were faced with reconciling Christians who had abandoned their faith during the persecutions, they realized what Jesus had meant that night. He had foreseen situations then facing them and had given them the power to reconcile sinners to God's grace.

When the time came, however, for Jesus to leave for good, he gathered them all together for last-minute in-structions before he ascended. They were still curious as to whether he intended "to restore the kingdom to Israel." Sidestepping the question, he said to them, "It is not for you to know the times or the dates that the Father has de-termined by his own authority. But as for yourselves, you will receive power when the Holy Spirit comes upon you. Then you will be my witnesses, not only in Jerusalem, but throughout Judea and Samaria, and indeed to the ends of the earth."

In spite of these assurances, after his departure at the As-cension, all the anxiety and panic returned, and they again went into hiding for fear of being arrested, going out only as need demanded. Ten days later, "on the Jewish feast of Pen-tecost, as they had all gathered together, all of sudden they heard what sounded like a powerful wind from heaven, the noise of which filled the entire house in which they were staying. Something then appeared to them that looked like tongues of fire, which then separated and came to rest on the head of each of them. They were all filled with the Holy Spirit, and began to speak foreign languages, as the Spirit gave them the gift of speech.

"Now, there were devout men living in Jerusalem, from every nation under heaven, and on hearing this sound, they all assembled. Each one was bewildered at hearing these men speaking in his own language. They were amazed and astonished. 'Surely,' they said, 'all these men speaking are Galileans. How can it be that each of us hears them in his own native language? Parthians, Medes, Elamites, people from Mesopotamia, Judea and, Cappodocia, Pontus and Asia, Phrygia and Pamphylia, Egypt, and parts of Libya round Cyrene, as well as visitors from Rome—Jews and proselytes alike, Cretans and Arabs; we have heard them preaching in our own language about the marvels of God.' Everyone was amazed and unable to explain it. They asked one another what it all meant."

That was the beginning. Other manifestations of the Holy Spirit followed in rapid succession. As one reads the Acts of the Apostles, one might easily assume, since Jesus had promised the Apostles that the Holy Spirit would be working through them, that the many miracles performed through the Apostles was the work of the Holy Spirit. The vast multitude of conversions is clearly a powerful demonstration of the Spirit's grace touching the hearts of so many at one time. Conversions were not easy in those days because people were putting their lives, their family, and their property on the line. The Spirit of God had to be at work in their hearts.

There were many occasions when Peter, filled with the Holy Spirit, got up and spoke to large crowds about Jesus and his message. Gone was all the old fear and insecurity. A bold new man now had the courage to speak out in the shadow of the temple and under the watchful eyes of the Pharisees and Sadducees, and the temple police.

One of the most powerful manifestations of the presence of the Holy Spirit working in the soul of an individual is the story of Stephen, the first martyr. After confessing his faith in Jesus as his Lord and Redeemer, and about to be stoned to death, Saint Luke writes in the Acts of the Apostles, "Stephen, filled with the Holy Spirit, gazed into heaven and saw the glory of God, and Jesus standing at God's right hand, 'I can see heaven thrown open,' he said, 'and the Son of Man standing at God's right hand.' "

Reading that passage over and over all one's life dulls the drama of the event. But the early Christians who either witnessed it, or even the bystanders who later turned to the Lord, were profoundly moved not only at Stephen's courage but by the awesome apparition that gripped the holy man as he was about to be stoned to death. Saint Luke was clearly moved by what people had experienced that day.

The Holy Spirit exerted a powerful presence among the first Christian community in Jerusalem. It was important to the Apostles that their disciples receive the Holy Spirit, and not just baptism. When the Apostles heard that the Samaritans had accepted Jesus, they sent Peter and John to them to tell them about the Holy Spirit, because as yet the Holy Spirit had not yet come down upon them. They had been baptized only in the name of the Lord Jesus. So they laid hands on them and they received the Holy Spirit. This laying on of hands was the manner in which authority and power was passed on from the Apostles to those chosen, either to receive spiritual gifts or the authority Jesus had given to them. That is why even today each bishop in the Church can trace his apostolic authority and responsibilities back to one of the Apostles.

Communicating his life and good news to the people was the command Jesus gave to his Apostles. They were the custodians of the treasures he brought to earth. Even calling down the Holy Spirit upon the disciples was the responsibility of the Apostles, so when Peter and John prayed over this group of Samaritans, and laid hands upon them, the Holy Spirit came to them in the same dramatic manifestation as the Apostles had experienced on Pentecost. Today we would call this the Sacrament of Confirmation in the Spirit. One might wonder why Jesus placed so much authority and responsibility on the Apostles, and did not just let people go to God directly, and pass on his message to one another, without official teachers, and without intermediaries to channel God's gifts. It becomes clear when one realizes that Jesus came not just to give a message but to gather us together into a family. Relating to God on our own and independently of one another was foreign to Jesus. He came to gather together his Father's family. This responsibility and authority he placed upon the Apostles and those they consecrated to continue their work by praying and the laying on of hands. It was for them to preach the message, to gather God's people together, to channel God's life to them in baptism and then call down upon them the Holy Spirit. This sharing in Jesus' divine life was the bond uniting his followers to one another, so they were no longer separate individuals worshiping God on their own, but bonded into a family with ties of love and caring for one another. By giving this authority to the Apostles and those who would one day take their place, Jesus guaranteed the continuation of his Father's family on earth. He also guaranteed the faithful transmission of his message in its integrity until the end of time. A powerful bond united the community, the bond that Jesus prayed for at the Last Supper: "Father, I pray that they may all be one, even as you and I are one, so the world may believe that you have sent me."

It was unthinkable that leaders would separate themselves from the Apostles, and gather their own followers to worship on their own and attempt to call down the Holy Spirit on their own disciples. In ancient times when the Samaritans, who were Israelites, had left the Jewish religion and started their own manner of worship, they had cut themselves off from the religious authority Yahweh had established. When the Samaritan woman asked Jesus where they should worship, Jesus was quick in his response. "You worship what you do not know. Salvation is from the Jews." He then went on to tell her that a whole new way of worshiping God was about to happen.

While the Holy Spirit guided the Church through the administration of the Apostles, there were others whom the Holy Spirit inspired with other gifts, like the man named Agabus. He had a reputation for prophecy, and on one occasion prophesied a famine would overtake the whole Empire of Rome. When this actually happened during the reign of Claudius, the Christian communities were stunned by the accuracy of the prophecy. As this particular community was rather well off, they sent Barnabas and Saul with contributions to the families in Judea, who were suffering greatly.

The Holy Spirit had been working powerfully among the young community of Jesus' followers in Antioch. Their numbers were increasing daily and their enthusiasm to spread Jesus' message was unlike that of any of the other churches. Among the disciples were a number of outstanding prophets and teachers. By name they were Barnabas, Simeon, Lucius of Cyrene, Menaen, who had been brought up with Herod the tetrarch, and Saul. One day, while worshiping, inspired by the Holy Spirit, they were told to set aside Barnabas and Saul to go out on the mission the Holy Spirit had chosen for them. With that, they laid their hands on them and sent them off to follow wherever the Holy Spirit would lead them, which ended up being Cyprus, where many came to know the Lord, then on to Antioch in Pisidia, where their ministry was most fruitful among the Jewish community.

Eight

"HE WILL BRING
BACK TO
YOUR MINDS . . ."

For years, while the Apostles were still alive, remarkable happenings occurred, which they attributed to the power of the Holy Spirit. By the time the last Apostle died, there were already tens of thousands of followers of Jesus, none of them steeped in theology as we know it, none of them steeped in the New Testament as we know it. As there was no printing press in those days, most Christians were not even familiar with the Gospels or the other books of the New Testament. That did not mean that they were uninformed. They were instructed by word of mouth in what was important for them to know. They were powerfully instructed into the life, sufferings, death, and resurrection of Jesus as recounted so vividly to them by the Apostles. It was left to their successors to develop on the foundation of the Apostles. In time, a number of highly educated Greek, Roman and, African philosophers accepted Jesus' message. Many of them were consecrated bishops who were appointed to lead their local Christian communities. Their inquisitive minds needed to know more precisely just who this Jesus was. Was he God? Was he a human God like their Greek and Roman gods, or was his body just an illusion? Was his human body like ours, with passions, needs, and feelings? They spent their lives trying to find answers. They needed to understand just what "Son of God" really meant. In time they began to focus on the meaning of Three Persons in God.

The Holy Spirit now began to occupy a much more critical role in the Christian community, though not as obvious or as prominent a role as in the time of the Apostles. No more miracles, no more raising the dead to life, no more tearing open prison gates to free imprisoned Apostles, all of which was needed to show open minds that God was indeed behind this Jesus and his teachings, and endorsing the teaching of his disciples. The Holy Spirit would still perform the work Jesus promised he would do, but in a different way. "I will send to you the Holy Spirit who will bring back to your minds all the things that I have taught you." It now became the ever-increasing role of the Spirit to guide the *mind* of the Church, ensuring that Jesus' original message would not only be understood in its integrity but developed and explained to those who needed a deeper understanding of Jesus and who he was. Questions like "Who was this Jesus? Is he really still alive? If he is still alive, where does he live? In heaven, or is he still with us in some way? What is this baptism we receive? Is it just a symbol, or does something happen inside us when we are baptized? What does it do to us? What is this meal we eat, this Eucharist whom we are told is his flesh and blood? Is it really his flesh and blood, or is it just a symbol? Is he really with us when we receive him in Eucharist? How is Jesus related to God the Father? How is he related to the Holy Spirit? Are they really only one, or are there three Gods?" These were questions intelligent minds needed to have answered in some way. And that was all right. Did not Saint Peter tell the earlier disciples who had similar, though simpler questions, to find a reason for their faith?

Fortunately, there was no lack of great minds among the next generation of Jesus' disciples. Many Greek, Roman, African, and Syrian philosophers embraced Jesus' way of life. A number of them became bishops, some of them consecrated by the Apostles themselves. They were well equipped to probe the mysteries of Jesus' identity and teachings. Their brilliance was needed to formulate in succinct statements what Jesus taught, and to answer questions of intelligent nonbelievers interested in learning more about God and Jesus, and his teachings. This meant grappling with profound philosophical and theological issues. The next three centuries were driven by inevitable controversy, which rose from intelligent minds trying to understand what was a new phenomenon in the human experience. On the surface these heated and not too charitably driven controversies might seem scandalous to observers from our time. However, such precise analyses of Jesus' teachings, and indeed, of his person itself, was critical to an understanding, though always inadequate, of the nature of God and his Incarnate Son, and what this new religion was offering to its followers: an intimate relationship with God who loves his creatures, and the promise of life after death to those who are faithful.

Jesus had promised to be with the Apostles until the end of time and to send the Holy Spirit to bring back to their minds all that he had taught. This was the time and these were the circumstances when that guidance was sorely needed. The endless discussions and hotly debated questions about Jesus and his teachings absorbed the Christian communities in the East and West for over two hundred years. Cynical minds of today view all these matters as petty political issues. These issues were far from being merely political, though powerful political figures involved themselves in matters of the Church, since such matters could unite or polarize the populace. The central figures in the debates, however, were saintly men deeply concerned about the nature of the Son of God, and how they could explain with accuracy to the Christian people, and to pagans, just who this God-Man was. Final dogmatic definitions of Jesus' identity and other issues were decided on purely theological and scriptural grounds. Even today those definitions are admired, not only for their fidelity to scripture and traditional beliefs, but for their precision in expression and brilliance in their clarity, like finely polished diamonds.

Besides the issues surrounding Jesus' identity, and the nature of God as Three Persons, there were other more pragmatic concerns. The community of Christians was growing into vast numbers. They could no longer meet in people's houses or in small groups. They now met in what was called gatherings. A gathering was called a "church," or *ekklesia* in Greek. As the Apostles died, others took their places. These men chosen by the Apostles to succeed them were not called apostles, though they assumed the same authority and power that Jesus had given to the Apostles. Their role was identical with that of the Apostles. Their new title was *episkopos*, bishop. They and the deacons were officials, or *presbyteroi*, in these *ekklesias*, or church communities. Prophets were also prominent. Though it was the function proper to the bishops to celebrate the Eucharist, prophets were allowed to celebrate Eucharist. The new churches were evolving from the simple organizational structure of their early beginnings into a more efficient model better suited to meet ever-changing conditions. During these changes, the leaders were strongly conscious of the presence and guidance of the Holy Spirit. They knew that Jesus had guided and instructed the Apostles when he was on earth. Now that he was gone, they looked to the Holy Spirit for that same guidance and direction. Assured of this, they made necessary decisions boldly. They did not yet have cannonized scripture to guide them, nor set theological principles. The authority Jesus gave them depended totally on the Spirit's inspiration, and their trust in that inspiration was total.

As the community grew, formulas of faith were needed.

Stories from the life of Jesus, and from what he said, were no longer adequate. They demanded understanding of what Jesus meant. Those interpretations were fast in coming, first from the Apostles themselves, then from their immediate successors.

Some of these clarifications involved an understanding of baptism, the breaking of bread, the positions in the community of those with special gifts and responsibilities, and even more important, the place of the individual in relation to the community as God's family. Requirements of faith were simple in the beginning: belief in God, the all-powerful ruler of the universe, and in his beloved Son, Jesus, the Savior of the human race, who was born of the Holy Spirit by the Virgin Mary. He lived and died, rose from the dead, and ascended into heaven. He now sits at the right hand of God and will be the Judge of the living and the dead. Primitive faith also included belief in the Holy Spirit, the Giver of life, and belief in the Church as God's family, with the Apostles and their successors as appointed by God to guide and govern the Church. Those beliefs were incorporated into Creeds, or statements, of beliefs. There were, however, other objects of belief that were part of the Christian's life, like confession of sins before receiving the Eucharist, so their offering to God would be pure, belief in the Eucharist as the flesh and blood of Jesus, so sacred that Communion could not be given to anyone who had not been baptized, and belief that only the Apostles and their successors were empowered by Jesus to celebrate, or consecrate, the Eucharist. The Apostles made an exception of authentic prophets, and empowered them to celebrate Eucharist for the community. It was also essential that individuals not worship independently of the Church, as the Church was the family Jesus established, and worship should be performed as a family if it was to be pleasing to God.

As the Church grew, the numbers alone demanded more efficient organization as well as an even greater clarity and explanation of beliefs, as strange interpretations and theories about Jesus began to proliferate. Frequently, these ideas were far from reality. One theory held that the humanity of Jesus was only an appearance of bodily form. For these believers, called Docetists (from the Greek *dokein*, "to seem"), anything material was evil, including the human body. It was for them repulsive for Jesus to have a body made of earthly matter. Following from this belief was the idea that Jesus' sufferings were not real, but imaginary. This served only to push Jesus far out of reach of people who were trying to draw near to God. Among those promoting this heresy were the Gnostics, and later, the Pelagians. Saint Ignatius, the bishop of Antioch, and one of the few still alive who, as a young man, knew Jesus, fought strongly against this theory. In one of his letters he writes, "But, as some atheists, that is, unbelievers, say, his suffering was make believe. These people hold back from Eucharist and prayer because they do not confess that the Eucharist is the Flesh of our Savior Jesus Christ, which suffered for our sins, and which the Father in his loving kindness raised from the dead." In another place he refers to the Eucharist as "the medicine of immortality, the antidote against death, and everlasting life in Jesus Christ."

From this controversy, the doctrine developed that Jesus' body was a real human body, and not a phantom, or make-believe body, and that the Eucharist makes his presence real to us. From that one teaching alone a whole set of beliefs grew. Jesus was really and truly one of us. He understood our humanity. He shared our pain, our suffering. He knew temptation, and understood our weakness. "He was," as Saint Paul said, "like us in all things but sin." This doctrine of the Church that Jesus is one of us and understands us has been the source of tremendous comfort to millions of suffering and troubled souls through the centuries. The development of this understanding of Jesus shows graphically what Jesus meant when he said he would send the Holy Spirit to help the Apostles and their successors to understand more fully all that he taught. When people criticize the Church for its dogmas and doctrines and say that we do not need dogma and we do not need doctrine, all we need is Jesus, they are so wrong. Understanding Jesus *is* doctrine. The more fully doctrine is developed, the more completely we understand the real Jesus. And it is this understanding, guided by the Holy Spirit's wisdom, that inspires the Church to make Jesus real again in our lives, through its teaching and through its sacraments, especially the Eucharist.

Saint Ignatius' life is also a remarkable testimony to the unique spirituality and mysticism that grew from intimacy with the risen Jesus. It shows in an extraordinary way how the Holy Spirit was fulfilling his role of molding Jesus in the lives of his followers. Molding Jesus in the lives of Christians is the forgotten work of the Holy Spirit, especially in our own day. Yet it was intended to be, and has always been, the essential work of the Spirit. What else is Christianity, if not the transformation of human beings into God's children, modeled after Jesus' own life? "Come, follow me. I am the way, the truth, and the life," Jesus said. Reading the life of Saint Ignatius of Antioch is a marvelous experience. He was an old man when he was dragged off on a Roman ship to the imperial city to be martyred. His life had always been, in a very special way, modeled on Jesus'. He was concerned, however, that although he had struggled so hard to be like the Master, he was concerned about one thing especially. Jesus had given his life for us, and he had not yet given his life for Jesus. He looked forward with joy to the time when he could die a martyr, even though it meant being destroyed in a public circus by wild beasts. He was a rare saint in the early days of Christianity, a warm, gentle man whom Christians from all the churches loved and venerated. His teachings and admonitions have that ring of authenticity as mirroring the mind of Jesus himself.

The spirituality and mysticism of Saint Ignatius was responsible for the growth of Christian mysticism in the earliest centuries of Christianity. Vastly different from the mysticism of the Far East, it was characterized by intimacy with the presence of God and Jesus within the soul of the individual, already prepared by the Holy Spirit's gentle action within the person. It is an entirely new type of mysticism, which was to flourish not only in the early days of Christianity but in the later medieval monasteries, at the time the Church was considered by some to be so corrupt and materialistic. Saint Ignatius saw Jesus as the intimate companion of the committed Christian, the source of his life, and the Church as the family among which Jesus was always present, and most powerfully present as the Church gathered in worship. Where the bishop is, there is Christ. To cut oneself off from the bishop or work independently of one's bishop is to cut oneself off from Christ himself.

Already, after only sixty or seventy years, we can see the Church growing in depth and breadth, not only in membership, but in self-understanding and greater awareness of the mystery that Jesus had entrusted to it. The Church, under the gentle guidance of the Spirit, was developing a life of its own. It was becoming truly the Mystical Body of Jesus, and the living presence of God on earth, transforming, as Jesus promised, the whole civilization around it. It was the yeast in the dough that raised the level of human life into a new and supernatural dimension. This did not mean that the Church was impervious to human weakness or corruption among its members. That always will be, as long as the Church is doing its work faithfully and welcoming sinners into its family. A family of sinners will be at best dysfunctional in many ways, not only among the simple faithful, but among the shepherds themselves. Painful as it is to those who love the Church as Jesus' great gift, it is reality. Jesus' parables of the kingdom revealed in a brutally realistic way that earthy reality. He spoke of the kingdom on earth as the "pearl of great price," but then in the next breath, as "the field of wheat in which the enemy had sown weeds."

The Church, now in full bloom, was beginning to show its emerging spiritual genius as well as its shameful human failings. Within hardly a hundred years, as the philosophers embraced Christianity, they tied together in logical and intelligent fashion the various teachings of Jesus. They thus presented to a hostile pagan world, a defense of the faith that could stand up honorably against the prevalent philosophical systems. And it was not in vain. Many other educated persons embraced Jesus, and by the late second century, Jesus' followers had formed a powerful subculture throughout the empire. They had become, as Jesus foresaw, the yeast in the dough, causing the whole of society to rise to new and unknown levels of morality and goodness. Great and bold men made powerful contributions to popularize the faith, both at the imperial court as well as among the educated: Quadratus, who addressed an explanation of Christian life and teachings to the Emperor Hadrian; and Justin, who had been a Pythagorean philosopher; and the Athenian philosopher, Aristides, who also wrote a treatise on Christianity to the Emperor Hadrian; and Athenagoras of

Athens, the most polished and eloquent of the early apologists, who addressed an explanation of the faith to the emperors Marcus Aurelius Antoninus and Lucius Aurelius Commodus, the son of Emperor Marcus Aurelius. In their writings, these and other apologists developed a way of explaining to learned pagans the teachings of Jesus, and the religious practices of Christians.

By far the most important of the early Church fathers was Irenaeus, bishop of Lyons, who was born most probably in Asia Minor. His teachings on the relationship between God the Father and Jesus is an important first step into understanding something of the mystery of the Trinity, which he admits is indescribable, and not only indescribable, but incomprehensible to the human mind. Irenaeus also found the role of Mary as critical to our redemption. As he says, because Mary was obedient to God, unlike Eve, she became the cause of salvation both to herself and the human race, in the same way as Eve became the cause of our calamity by her disobedience to God.

Irenaeus also probes the relationship between God and human beings. Humans are made to the image of God. But Irenaeus recognizes in Adam and Eve a deeper relationship with God. Since God shared his life with them, he thereby enhanced his image in their being, not by deification, but by some mystical identification. This was accomplished by the power of the Holy Spirit. The same happens to Christians. It is in the sacraments that redemption is effected. A creature receives its perfection in the sacraments. By baptism we are born again to God, "For he came to save all through means of himself, all I say, who through him are born again to God, infants, and children, boys and youths, and old men" (against heretics). This image of God in the souls of Christians is enhanced by the sacraments, especially baptism, for the life of God is infused into the soul, making them truly children of God, not by mere adoption, but by infusion of his life.

What is so noticeable in wandering through the writings of the earliest Christians is the gradual and subtle development in understanding of all that Jesus taught, just as he had promised. Again, these ideas are not products of a human mind. Each of these writers makes a simple statement that in itself does not seem so significant, and whose importance they may not have even realized, but putting them all together, each one's contribution shows a dramatic advance in fleshing out the sublime teachings of the Master. One can sense the subtle promptings of the Holy Spirit, as one by one, a new insight into God's nature is introduced, providing, over a period of time, a clearer understanding of

God, of his relationship to the Son and the Holy Spirit, as well as God's inestimable love for his human creatures. Irenaeus was deeply taken up with the mystery of the Church, which for him was the chosen vessel of truth guaranteeing the integrity of Jesus' message until the end of time. For him, the Church cannot depart from the truth of Jesus' teachings. "Wherefore it is essential to obey the presbyters, who are in the Church, those whom I have shown possess the succession from the Apostles; those who together with the succession of the episcopate, have received the certain gift of truth according to the good pleasure of the Father. (From his "Discourse Against Heretics") This guarantee of the integrity of Jesus' teachings in the Church comes from the guidance of God's Spirit. Heretics have no assurance of the truth of what they teach because they cut themselves off from the bishops, the successors of the Apostles, and therefore, from the guidance of the Holy Spirit.

A letter written by an unknown author to a prominent Roman official by the name of Diognetus, who may have been the tutor of Marcus Aurelius, defines, in a way that seems almost inspired, what a Christian is:

" 'Who is the God in whom they trust,' you wonder, 'and what kind of cult is theirs to enable them, one and all, to disdain the world and despise death, and neither to

recognize the gods believed in by the Greeks nor to practice the superstition of the Jews? And what is the secret of
that strong affection they have for one another? And why
has this new blood or spirit come into the world we live in
now, and not before?'"

He then goes on to describe the supernatural life of
Christians: "Christians are not distinguished from the rest
of mankind by either country, speech, or customs; the fact
is, nowhere do they settle in cities of their own; they use
no peculiar language; they cultivate no eccentric mode of
life. Certainly, this creed of theirs is no discovery due to
some conceit or speculation of inquisitive men; nor do
they, as some sects do, champion any doctrine of human
origin. Yet, while they settle in both Greek and non-
Greek cities, as each one's lot is cast, and conform to the
customs of the country in dress, diet, and mode of life in
general, the whole tenor of their way of living stamps it as
worthy of admiration and admittedly contrary to expecta-
tion. They reside in their respective countries, but only as
aliens; they take part in everything as citizens, and put up
with everything as foreigners; every foreign land is their
home, and every home is a foreign land. They marry like
all others, and beget children; but they do not expose their
offspring. Their board they spread for all, but not their

bed. They find themselves in the flesh, but do not live according to the flesh. They spend their days on earth, but hold citizenship in heaven. They obey the established laws, but in their private lives go beyond the laws. They love all men, and are persecuted by all. They are unknown, yet are condemned; they are put to death, and are restored to life. They are poor and enrich many, destitute of everything, they abound in everything. They are dishonored, and in their dishonor find their glory. They are calumniated, and are vindicated. They are reviled, and they bless; they are insulted and render honor. Doing good, they are penalized as evildoers; when penalized, they rejoice because they are quickened into life. The Jews make war on them as men of a different tribe; the Greeks persecute them; and those who hate them can assign no reason for their enmity.

"To say it briefly: what the soul is to the body, that Christians are to the world. The soul is spread through all the members of the body, and the Christians throughout all the cities of the world." The author then goes on to say that as the soul of the world the goodness of their lives holds the world together, and though they live in corruptible bodies like everyone else, they look forward when one day they will be incorruptible in heaven. How Jesus' small group of disciples had grown, and what a powerful impression they made on society. They had become, indeed, the yeast in the dough raising the level of life throughout a pagan world.

The growth in understanding the simple message of Jesus is so impressive that one cannot help but realize that Jesus did keep his promise to send the Holy Spirit to be with the Church and enlighten it to a fuller realization of what he taught. Reading the early Fathers of the Church, one senses that influence of the Holy Spirit, more so on some of the Fathers than on others. In the later part of the second century, there arose a man whose life was filled with God's Spirit in a way that affected the whole Christian world and even beyond. His name was Origen. He was born in A.D. 185 into a large Christian family, in Alexandria, Egypt. When he was seventeen years old, his father, Leonidas, was arrested and martyred for his faith. His son, who wanted so much to be martyred with his father, tried to go with him, but his mother had hidden his clothes and prevented him from leaving the house. Humorous as it may seem, it saved his life, a life that was to be filled with incredible creativity. He is without doubt the most voluminous writer in all of history, having written over six thousand works. Christian literature took a

giant leap as a result of Origen's career. Origen lived close
enough to the time of the Apostles to be influenced by
men who were children of the Apostles' immediate disciples. He had an intimate knowledge of how the earliest
Christians lived and what was important to them. He was
not only knowledgeable in the Hebrew scriptures and
Christian literature, but being fluent in Greek, Hebrew,
and Latin, he drew on all these sources when composing
his own works. They are masterpieces. As today, so in
Origen's time, various interpretations of Jesus' teachings
began to spring up, causing confusion and conflict in the
Christian communities. Origen's solution was simple,
which he explains in his *First Principles*. "Since many,
however, of those who profess to believe in Christ differ
from each other, not only in small and trifling matters, but
also on subjects of the highest importance, . . . it seems on
that account necessary first of all to fix a definite limit and
to lay down an unmistakable rule regarding each one of
these, and then to pass to the investigation of other points
. . . as the teaching of the Church, transmitted in orderly
succession from the Apostles, and remaining in the
churches to the present day, is still preserved, that alone is
to be accepted as truth which differs in no respect from ec-
clesiastical and apostolic tradition" (Pref. 1–2 ANF).

Origen's life was extraordinary as well. Eusebius, the great historian, was struck with the influence and holiness of Origen's life. He was a man in whom the Spirit of God worked powerfully, and drew many others to the Christian way of life.

Unique for the times was Origen's total immersion in Jesus' life. His spirituality, though similar to that of Irenaeus, was much more intense. Origen had, from his early boyhood, a strong attraction to God and spirituality. His prayer life flowed from an intimacy with God, which made God as real for him as his best friend. From his writings one can easily detect that he was blessed with rare insights into the mind of God, the teachings of Jesus, and the Christian life. These insights, no doubt, were the basis for many of his creative ideas, as they were far advanced for the period in which he lived. He talks of Jesus, the Logos, as *homoousios* ("of the same substance") with God the Father. That is the same term that theologians were to use almost a hundred years later in defining the relationship between God the Father and the Son. He refers to Mary as *Theotokos*, the Mother of God, though the term was not to be used officially for another hundred years, and then only after violent debates. Also he speaks of the motherhood of Mary as embracing the whole Christian family. "No one may understand the meaning of the Gospel (of Saint John), if he has not rested his head on the breast of Jesus and received Mary from Jesus to be his mother also" (from his commentary on St. John's Gospel).

Thoughts he shares in his writings on the spiritual life are very similar to expressions used by the medieval mystics, which would lead one to believe he had the same mystical experiences they enjoyed. Early Christians followed Jesus' teachings, but Origen's understanding is so much more profound and intimate than that of his contemporaries. For Origen, the highest good for a Christian, and, indeed, for everyone, is "to become as like to God as possible."

He then goes on to guide the soul into the way of following Jesus perfectly. Detachment from the world, and even from loved ones, is necessary if one is to follow God. Not that we are free of obligations to loved ones, but excessive emotional attachment can distract the soul trying to live in intimacy with God. As the soul grows in prayer, God, the Trinity, comes and dwells within, and shares knowledge and insights into many things. Gradually, the soul begins to think like God, and grows more and more to resemble the divine presence within.

He counsels that the soul that follows the way of perfection has many trials and temptations, and suffers much. But passing through these periods of painful experiences, the soul eventually enters into a mystical union with the Word of God, the Logos, and there experiences the ecstasy of divine love, with all the intimacy of God's tenderness toward the soul that has found him. It is in this state that God shares with this chosen soul understanding of the most complicated mysteries, and most difficult problems. For this soul all things become simple and comprehensible, as the mind becomes enlightened by God's own understanding.

As one reads the writings of the Fathers of the Church, it is difficult not to be impressed with the power of God working vividly on the minds of these holy people as they open their hearts to his Spirit. Never before in human history has such giant strides been made, not only in understanding God, but in developing intimacy with God, an intimacy that is not forced or make-believe, but authentic. The prophets of old, especially Moses, had intimacy with God, but it was always a frightening, awe-inspiring experience, as God placed heavy burdens upon them. This new kind of intimacy Origen speaks of comes from the new life of grace that Jesus won for us, and that is open to all who have embraced the Redeemer and his message of love.

And did not Jesus promise such? "If someone welcomes me, my Father and I will come and live within that person." And to come within, means to be alive within that person, to share God's vision and God's love, until gradually the soul sees and loves the way God sees and loves, until it becomes identified with God. It is the sole purpose of Christianity: to transform God's children into perfect images of his Goodness and Godliness.

Nine

"THE POWERS OF HELL SHALL NOT PREVAIL AGAINST IT."

A common theme in the writings of most of the early Fathers of the Church in both the East and the West was the sacred character of the Church. There were many who, for various reasons, broke from the Church. Toward these the Fathers were not very charitable. In fact, they were stinging in their denunciation of what they had done. "How can you call yourselves Christians when you have departed from Christ?" was the common theme among them. "In the Church there is Christ. In the Church there are the Apostles. In the Church there is Peter, the one on whom Jesus founded his Church. How can you leave this and say you are loyal to Christ?"

And yet, the Fathers had their differences with church authority. Saint Cyprian, bishop of Carthage, in the middle of the third century, had a very difficult time with the Pope of the time, Pope Stephen. When Cyprian insisted on rebaptizing apostate Christians returning to the faith after the persecutions, the Pope wrote a scathing letter to him, directing him to stop the practice, as it was not the tradition handed down from earliest times. Have them confess and do penance, yes, but do not have them rebaptized. Cyprian replied in a strongly worded letter, telling the Pope he respected him as the Bishop of Rome and the successor of Saint Peter, but also reminding him that he too was a successor of one of the Apostles and that the Pope should never again interfere in the running of his diocese. As strongly as he believed in his own authority as a successor of one of the Apostles, he believed just as strongly in the role of Peter's successor, though he felt the Pope should respect the autonomy of other bishops' decisions on how they run their dioceses. The two holy men died shortly afterward; Cyprian as a martyr.

As the instrument of Jesus' salvation, the Church had to be continually on guard against ideas that would confuse or undermine Jesus' message. Those ideas and theories were not long in coming. Arius, a priest from Alexandria, Egypt, denied the divinity of Jesus, saying that since the Son of God was begotten, God the Father had to exist before him. The Son then could not be God, but could be considered only as the firstborn of God's creatures. This heresy haunted the Church for decades, with even emperors taking sides. Saint Athanasius, at the time a deacon, and later the bishop of Alexandria, was the staunchest defender of the divinity of Jesus. He was relentless in promoting the idea that Jesus and God the Father were one, with one and the same essence, as the philosophers would say. He used the term that Origen used so many years before, *homoousion* ("of the same nature" or "essence"). Jesus was of the same essence as the Father. Others were willing to say that the Father and the Son were *homoiousion* ("of similar essence" or "nature"), which would mean that the Son might be similar to God, but not really divine. As Arius' friends among the powerful bishops in the East had the ear of the Emperor Constantine, Arius won the day. The emperor had a warrant sent out for Athanasius' arrest, but he managed always to outwit the troops sent to arrest him. His life reads like a novel. At one point in the controversy, so many clergy agreed with Arius that one bishop made the remark, "One morning we woke up and found the whole world had turned Arian." Except of course, Athanasius.

His persistence earned him the title "*Athanasius contra mundum*," "Athanasius against the world." However, his dogged determination prevailed after many years of struggle.

In the year A.D. 325 the first ecumenical council of the Church was convened by Emperor Constantine, who insisted that the bishops settle the matter once and for all. It was not only good for the Church; it was good for the Empire itself to have the people at peace.

The council strongly agreed with the Pope, Saint Celestine I, that Jesus was the Son of God, and that although he was begotten of the Father, there was no point at which the Son did not exist. He was always coeternal with the Father. They were both of the same substance (*homoousios*), and therefore One in being. The Son is truly God, as the Father is truly God. Arius, and two of his bishops, refused to accept the decision of the council, so they were exiled. Though the matter was officially decided, the controversy still continued for another fifty years, until the Council of Constantinople in 381, which finally ended the matter.

The next great controversy was over the person of Jesus. Did he have two natures—one human, the other divine? Or did he have only one nature—a fusion of the human and the divine? Were there two persons in Jesus—one divine, one human? Nestorius, a monk of Antioch, who later became archbishop of Constantinople, taught that in Jesus there were two *natures*—one human, one divine; but they were joined in a unique metaphysical union. He also believed that there were two *persons* in Jesus: one human and one divine. He taught that Mary, the Mother of Jesus, was only the mother of the human person in Jesus, so she should not be called the Mother of God, or *Theotokos*, as she was referred to by the common people, but only *Christotokos*, the Christ-bearer. This caused widespread resentment among the people, which occasioned the convening of the council of the whole Church, the Council of Ephesus. Under the guidance again of Pope Saint Celestine I, the council finally decided after much-heated debate that in Jesus there were two natures—one human, one divine, but united in only one person, the divine Person of the Son of God. Since a mother gives birth to a person, not just a body or a soul, and since Jesus' person was divine, Mary could truly be called *Theotokos*, or the Mother of God.

When the decision was made, late in the evening, the people of Ephesus went wild with joy, parading the streets of the city with torches, singing and dancing in wild acclamation.

What Jesus had taught in seed form was being expanded and elucidated through painful struggles as the Holy Spirit carried out his mission to make clear all the things that Jesus had taught to the Apostles.

Ten

"WE WILL COME AND LIVE WITHIN YOU."

T hough the great heresies concerning the identity of Jesus had become part of history, there were others of lesser concern that sprang up at various intervals. However, these were resolved rather calmly, and the Church found itself in relative peace. In the calm shortly after the Council of Ephesus, when people had more time to think about their own personal lives, a widespread interest in spirituality evolved, starting in Italy. Around A.D. 500, Saint Benedict gathered a small group of friends around himself who, like himself, were willing to dedicate their lives to prayer and penance. In a short period of time others were attracted to his way of life, and before long there were almost a dozen groups in various nearby places living the simple life of monks. Trying to bring some sense of order to their lives, Benedict gathered all his followers together and built a monastery big enough to accommodate all his companions. This first monastery was built on the peak of Monte Cassino in Italy, and became the real beginning of monastic life in Western Europe. Benedict's way of life became so popular, it soon spread throughout Italy and into other countries. Monasteries were not new. There were monasteries already existing in Greece, Syria, Egypt, Palestine, and what is now Lebanon. However, in the West, early on they sprung up in vast numbers, as thousands of people were drawn to this form of dedication to God. Not only were men attracted to monastic life, but women as well. Saint Benedict's sister, Saint Scholastica, insisted on having a monastery for women, which she soon set up under her brother's guidance. Over the next five hundred years there were over ten thousand monasteries of various religious orders in existence throughout Europe, filled with monks and nuns of varying degrees of holiness and spirituality. As time went on many became lax, and the monks lived lives of comfort, but reforms were constantly introduced to bring them back to their original ideals. For the most part, these monasteries became centers of learning and scholarship, and made vast contributions to the development of western civilization. They also provided the scholars who taught at the universities that bishops established throughout Europe. By the twelfth century there were over thirty universities flourishing in Italy, Spain, and France alone. Most of the teachers came from the monasteries. The University of Paris alone had over 50,000 students. These monasteries continued to play an important role in the academic and spiritual life of Europe until the Reformation, some two hundred years later, when in newly Protestant countries, the majority of them were disbanded, and the universities were confiscated or closed.

Reading stories of those times, one can see the tremendous burst of learning, culture, and spirituality. But alongside such greatness is the frightful immorality. No doubt that will always be the human condition, but it is painful to see such evil in the midst of what is clearly the Spirit of God working powerfully in the lives of so many, attempting to raise the level of spirituality and culture in a whole civilization.

The Church has had such a tumultuous history. Not only was it plagued by heresy and schism, but it was attacked from without by barbarian hordes, and at times even by Christian armies. What was most threatening, however, was not what was happening from without, but what was happening within. It had never been made clear how Peter's successors should be elected. As a result, powerful and unscrupulous nobles soon learned how to control the election of Popes and place their own cronies in the Chair of Peter. This caused untold harm to the Church and to the Christian people, to say nothing of the damage done to the reputation of the Church. Added to this was the immoral lifestyle of some of the clergy, and even of some of the Popes, though, fortunately, not more than five or six of the 262 in the almost 2,000-year history of the Church. Interestingly enough, as bad as they were, they never officially decreed anything that was heretical. With all the attacks on the Church from within and without, it is a miracle the Church survived. Other kingdoms, other religions, other denominations when encountering internal division and corruption, have come and gone, or have survived in certain limited areas of the world, but the Church continued to grow stronger and more widespread with the passage of time, until eventually it found itself in practically every country of the world. It could only be attributed to the powerful influence of the Holy Spirit, guiding the Church to preach to all nations as Jesus promised, and preserving it even in its most shameful periods.

Eleven

"AN ENEMY HAS COME AND SOWN WEEDS."

Throughout the history of the Church, alongside very human weaknesses, when the Church was shaken to its core by its laxity, there were powerful spiritual forces at work, inspiring not just monks and nuns, but cardinals, bishops, priests, and ordinary people to live lives not just of ordinary goodness but of heroic holiness. Martin Luther is perhaps the most immediately recognizable but others include: Saint Benedict the Moor, born of African slaves in Sicily, who later became a hermit and founded his own monastery and was noted for his humility and dedication to prayer and charity; Saint Charles Borromeo and Saint Robert Bellarmine (both cardinals and both towering giants of sanctity); Saint Philip Neri, who lived as a simple priest in Rome, founded a congregation to care for pilgrims and the sick, as well as an association of priests in Rome dedicated to the spiritual life, and preaching inspiring sermons; Saint Catherine of Siena, counselor to Popes, continually pressuring them to be faithful to Jesus' ideals; Saint Rose of Lima, the first canonized saint of the Americas, known for her extraordinary holiness and mystical experiences; Saint Martin de Porres, also from Lima, known for his care of the slaves and the poor; Benedict Canfield, martyred for his faith; Cardinal Pierre de Berulle, most outstanding spiritual director in France, dedicated to reform, who brought Saint Teresa of Ávila's Carmelites to France; Erasmus, a Dutch reformer, who corresponded with Martin Luther during his troubles, encouraging him to moderation; Saint Louis Bertrand, a Spanish Dominican friar who dedicated his life to the indigenous people of South America and was noted for his gift of prophecy; Saint Bernardino of Siena, a Franciscan priest noted for his inspiring sermons promoting moral reform; John Bessarion, a saintly Greek Catholic bishop who spent his life trying to heal wounds between Greece and Rome; Domingo Banes, a saintly Spanish theologian and confessor to Saint Teresa of Ávila, who fought tirelessly for justice for the indigenous peoples in the Americas; Gabriel Biel, a member of the Brethren of the Common Life, and a scholastic theologian, whose ideas impressed Luther as a student; Saint Angela Merici, who, after receiving a vision, founded an order of religious women dedicated to teaching young girls (her order, the Ursvlines, still exists today); Saint Francis Borgia, who resigned as Viceroy of Catalonia after his wife's death, established several colleges, and then became a Jesuit, spending his life promoting Christian ideals among the people; Saint Cajetan, who founded an order of priests dedicated to the spiritual life of the clergy and caring for the sick and the poor; Saint Camillus de Lellis, founder of the Camillians, who dedicated their lives to founding hospitals and caring for the sick; their hospitals are still widespread; Saint Aloysius Gonzaga, the young Jesuit seminarian who died of the black plague while nursing the sick. These were a mere few of the outstanding ones, but the list seems endless. From reading biographies of saints from that period, it seems that at the time of Luther, there were more sainted bishops and clergy, as well as laypeople, involved in not only reform movements but in works of charity and in the development of spiritual and mystical life, than at any other time in the Church's history. This makes one wonder why some people choose to focus on the evil in the Church at the time, and ignore all the spirituality that was flourishing at the same time.

This interest in the spiritual life flowed from the realization of Jesus' desire to be forever close to his followers, not only in their prayer life but in their anguish and suffering. It was the vital force driving these people, and others through the ages to give up material possessions and prospects of worldly power and fame, and spend their life in prayer and penance, contemplation and works of mercy. Institutes of charity, colleges, universities, and monasteries established then still exist. While there were always monks and nuns, in the fourteenth, fifteenth, and sixteenth centuries, an interest in the mystical life blossomed. It is thrilling to read the lives of such mystics as Saint Teresa of Ávila, Saint John of the Cross, Saint Philip Neri, and Saint Bernard of Clairvaux. Again, nothing like this has ever been experienced in such vast numbers and quality of the sanctity in all of human history. And when the Church splintered in the sixteenth century, supposedly for noble reasons, there were still thousands of saintly monks and nuns, as well as laypeople, involved in reform movements throughout the Church. The Brothers and Sisters of the Common Life are an example of the vibrant spiritual life among even the laypeople in the fourteenth and fifteenth centuries. By the mid-fifteenth century there were over a hundred houses of Brethren and Sisters, with over eighty monasteries, where they devoted their lives to the reading of scripture, contemplation, and copying devotional literature. Their distinctive form of spirituality was known as the "New Devotion," *Devotio Moderna*, emphasizing interior fervor and simple faith. They encouraged lay spirituality and supported the distribution of vernacular translations of the scriptures and devotional works among the people. This and other reform groups at the time had a significant effect on the spiritual life in the Church. Also at this time, Johannes Gutenberg, a member of the Franciscan third order, not only invented the printing press but printed the Bible for the first time, making possible wider distribution of the scriptures.

Reform was indeed needed, and was taking place. What was not needed was the tearing apart of Christendom, done in the name of reform, for mostly political reasons. Princes schemed to be independent of the Holy Roman Emperor, and demanded unquestioned control over the religion of their subjects. This was not reform. It was the worst form of abuse of power, wherein the state had total control over the people, and even over their minds.

Christianity is still struggling with the effects of that division, trying after four hundred years to heal the wounds it has caused throughout the Christian world.

But the finger of the Holy Spirit can still be seen in all the calamities that befell the Church. The Church had not entirely recovered from the experience of the Reformation than the French Revolution stripped the Church of all its universities, monasteries, hospitals, and orphanages. It was as if the Holy Spirit was purifying the Church and preparing it for a mission that would be needed to guide the world through challenging though difficult times to come, as social and industrial revolutions would shake the whole world.

During all this time, the Holy Spirit was still following Jesus' mandate, working powerfully and subtly in the hearts of sincere people, nudging them to find what had been lost during the time of past tragedies. Again all things must be made new in Christ. We see among people, and not just among Christians, a restlessness, a yearning, for deeper relationship with God. The longing seems to be much more widespread than at previous times. The external trappings of religion, or religious ceremonies alone, no longer satisfy the human spirit. People crave greater intimacy with the divine. And isn't that what religion is supposed to do for people: teach them how to draw close to the divine, and how to communicate through prayerful meditation and contemplation with the God who lives within us? After living an easy life until he was thirty-three years old, Saint Augustine finally found God, and in finding him, found peace and meaning to his life. It was then he made that famous observation, "Our hearts were made for you, O God, and they will rest only when they rest in you."

And that is the answer to the restlessness in people's hearts today. They need to find God if they are going to find the peace and forgiveness and healing that is so important in our modern world. It was precisely to offer us this peace and this forgiveness and healing that Jesus revealed to us the Trinity. It is the Trinity that works in the inner depths of our souls, drawing us into an ever sharper awareness of God, and helping us to understand the meaning of our lives.

Our souls are temples of the Trinity. As Sister Elizabeth of the Trinity, the modern Carmelite mystic, once said, "My soul is a heaven in which God dwells. I must learn to live there with him." This is a profound reality and gives new meaning and substance to our lives on earth. It is also the first principle of Christian spirituality, the indwelling of God's Spirit in those who open their hearts to him. It is a special gift that Jesus offered to those who accept him, and it is what makes Christian spirituality and mysticism essentially different from other forms of mysticism, which is often centered on self and oneness with nature.

I often wondered why Jesus spoke so often about himself and his Father being one, and how the Holy Spirit was so much a part of his life, and would be an intimate part of our lives, as well as the guide and protector of the Church. As I grew older I began to realize why it was important to Jesus that we know more fully what God is like and how he works in different ways within us and in the Church, and in the world at large. Because each person of the Trinity would have a special part to play in each of our lives and an essential element of those relationships was our own participation and cooperation. It was necessary for our bonding with each of the Persons of the Trinity. We look to God as a loving, caring Father who has sent his beloved Son to the world to redeem and save us. Jesus came among us as a friend and companion as well as our Redeemer and Savior. The Holy Spirit, as the Love between the Father and the Son, as the divine Love, is the intimate Partner in molding the divine within each of us, and the Partner in planning our day-to-day growth in holiness. He is, as Jesus told us, our Paraclete, our Comforter, our Consoler, our Friend, whose function is to mold the Image of Jesus in the Church and in the souls of individual Christians.

When Jesus revealed to us the nature of God as a Trinity of Persons, he was not revealing a theological concept. He was sharing with us his inner life. He was telling us about himself. He wanted us to be his friends. He was sharing himself with us so that our lives could be drawn into his life, into the intimacy of his love.

Twelve

"MY SOUL IS
A HEAVEN WHERE
GOD LIVES."

—Sr. Elizabeth of the Trinity, O.C.D.

After all the controversy over the centuries about the Trinity and the relationships of the divine Persons within the Trinity, a saintly writer once remarked, "I would rather experience the Trinity than be able to define it." Now that we know that God exists as a Trinity, how did Jesus intend that we incorporate this mystery of his inner life into our own lives, and into the life of the Church? That is what is really important to us. So often in my work as a priest, people ask me, "How should I pray?"

I never quite know what they are asking me, what they mean by it. I have always looked upon praying as a simple conversation with a God who cared even though he knew

I have made a lot of mistakes in my life. I am also aware that my way is not the only way to pray. There are many other ways, as people follow their own inclinations when talking to God. My father loved to pray the rosary. He could become deeply engrossed in God when he prayed the rosary. My mother like to talk to Jesus, and when she was worried or troubled about us kids, even when we were big kids, she would pray to the Blessed Mother, or pray the rosary.

In the life of that very simple saint, the Curé of Ars, he noticed that every day a peasant would go into the church and just sit in the bench, without ever saying anything. One day, out of curiosity, the Curé asked him, "Why do you come into church and just sit there, without saying any prayers?"

The simple man replied very simply, "I am not an educated man, Father. I don't know what to say to God. So I just look up at Jesus in the tabernacle, and Jesus looks at me. He knows I love him, and I know he loves me. That's the only way I know how to pray."

Some people like to read prayers from a book because they get distracted when they try to talk to God. Some like to look at a holy picture or a statue. It helps them to focus their thoughts because they do not know what to say. Their loving thoughts then are their prayers. Others like to ask God for all kinds of things that they feel are important for themselves and their friends and family. That is perfectly all right, too. Did not Jesus say "Whatever you ask the Father in my name he will grant you?"

There is a story in the life of the famous Italian writer Dante Alighieri, about one Sunday morning when he was at Mass. Dante had the habit of falling into ecstasy during Mass, totally absorbed. On this particular occasion, as the consecration prayers were being said, the whole congregation fell to their knees. All except Dante. The next day, he was summoned to the archbishop's palace.

The archbishop told him that people had complained to the archbishop's office that he had shown disrespect for the presence of Christ at Mass the previous day. When Dante asked the archbishop how he had shown disrespect, the archbishop replied, "At the consecration time, when everyone else knelt down, you remained standing. The people were shocked, and complained."

"Your excellency, I am sorry if I showed any disrespect. I was so caught up in the vision of Jesus on the altar, that I did not know what people were doing around me."

If we could be so caught up in the mystery of the sacred liturgy, we would find the real meaning of that beautiful gift that Jesus gave us. Many people, when they go to church, like to hear nice sermons, or pleasing music, or have a good experience in one way or another. There is nothing wrong with that. It is a good beginning. Dante's mind, however, was so filled with the wonder of the Mass, that as soon as he entered the church, his thoughts passed over all the sights and sounds around him, and he became focused on the mystery taking place beneath the surface of the ceremonies. He saw Jesus present on the altar, uniting everyone with himself as he offered himself to his heavenly Father. The presence of Jesus so absorbed his being, his every sense, that the actions of those around him ceased to be noticeable, ceased to be relevant.

Again, some people like to go off to a quiet place to pray, or walk in the woods. Still others can pray in the midst of crowds with no difficulty whatsoever. Some need books to pray, and find comfort in reading the prayers that others have composed. The authors seem to express so beautifully what these individuals are feeling but are unable to express by themselves.

All in all, everyone is different, with different personalities. Each one prays best when they follow the needs of their particular personality.

I think one of the most enjoyable ways of praying is

very simple. Find a special quiet time each day, any time of the day when it is peaceful. Take the Bible and open it up to the Gospels. You can either start at the beginning of Saint Matthew's Gospel, or take any part of any Gospel. Sit down, close your eyes, and ask the Holy Spirit to open your mind and your heart as you enter into your quiet time with God. Read a few paragraphs of whatever part you have chosen. Then sit back and relax. Now try to place yourself in the scene you have just read about, and try to understand what may have gone through Jesus' mind as he experienced that event, and also what the people were feeling; also what was going through the Apostles' minds, each one, including Judas. As you find yourself engrossed in this particular incident in Jesus' life, try to sense your own feelings about what is taking place, as if you are part of that event. What is your reaction to Jesus and to what he says, to what he does and to how he reacts to different people in the scene? Are you shocked at anything he says? Are you surprised by the way he talks to the scribes and Pharisees? To those looked upon by others as sinners?

After meditating for a period of time (you determine the length), spend some precious time alone in your thoughts with Jesus, or the Father, or the Holy Spirit; relate to whichever you feel drawn to at that particular time.

You will notice, after trying this a number of times, that you are beginning to develop a sense of closeness to Jesus, to the Father, and the Holy Spirit. You will also notice, as time goes by, that you are beginning to think differently, which will surprise you. You are beginning to think the way Jesus thinks. You are beginning to understand his attitudes toward different kinds of people and to issues you encounter in your own life.

When you finish this kind of prayer, thank God for the gift of grace that allows you to draw near to him. Now ask him for the grace that will enable you to apply to your life what you have learned in your meditation.

If you remain faithful to spending time each day in prayer like this, you will begin to sense a new intimacy with God that you never experienced before. You will feel as if God is right there with you. The emotions you feel will overwhelm you as you experience how beautiful and wonderful God is. This will encourage you to spend more time in this kind of prayer, because it is similar to falling in love. And it is really falling in love with God, as strange as it may seem. This intense emotion will also serve to intensify your prayer life, and make your meditations on the life of Jesus more real. You will now begin to understand what Saint Augustine meant when he said, "Our hearts were made for you, O God, and they will rest only when they rest in you." This resting in God's love is an experience entirely different from anything you may have known in the past. It is a small hint of the joy of being in heaven. But it is only a hint, and very emotional. There is more to come, which is even more beautiful and overwhelming, for those who persevere.

Thirteen

IF YOU WANT
TO FIND GOD,
LOOK WITHIN.

Jesus once said that if we love him and welcome him, he and his Father would come and live within us. What you are now experiencing as you commit to contemplative prayer is the fulfillment of Jesus' promise. He has come with his Father (and also the Holy Spirit) to dwell within you. That warm sense of the presence of God that you feel is not make-believe. It is God letting you know that he is there, right there within you, ready to be your Friend and your constant Companion. This intimacy that you are experiencing will most probably continue for months, perhaps, for even a longer period of time, until God feels you are ready for him to lead you into the next stage of your relationship with him. Remember, this kind of prayer leads you into a love relationship with God, so you will see many similarities to human love.

As you meditate each day on a different story in the Gospels, you gradually see different aspects of Jesus' personality. And remember, it is not just you meditating. It is also the Holy Spirit guiding you in your meditation, helping you to understand a little more of Jesus' life each day. This will begin to show in your life, in your relationships with others. You will look at people differently. You will look at them through Jesus' eyes. You will find yourself being more willing to listen to others, more interested in trying to understand them rather than being quick to judge them. Seeing the compassion in Jesus' life, you will notice that you are becoming more compassionate toward others.

However, there is a pitfall during this phase of your spiritual life. It has become so easy for you to be good, and to pray, and so enjoyable to live a spiritual life, you might begin to wonder why others cannot be the way you are. "Why cannot others be holy like me?" That is a trap so many fall into. It can be devastating. It was the trap the scribes and Pharisees fell into. They were basically good men, but they had become obsessed with their own goodness and pursuit of perfection. Seeing how good they had become, they began to look upon others with contempt. Jesus had a very difficult time with them, because they were so obnoxious. Jesus was not a fanatic in keeping the hundreds of their man-made religious laws, and the scribes and Pharisees accused him of showing contempt for the law.

So it is very important to avoid comparing others to yourself during this phase of your growth. A time will come when it will not be so easy for you to be good, and feel holy. For the time being, just be grateful that God has been so good to you. It is his gift that buoys you up and fills you with love for God, and for things spiritual. Learn all you can during these happy days and months. It will be a solid foundation for what you will experience later on, when the Holy Spirit takes you by the hand and leads you through a dark forest.

That dark forest will come when God has developed in you a strong attachment to Jesus, and to the Father. One day you will relax to meditate, and nothing will happen. You will read a passage of the Gospel, and within a few minutes you will fall off to sleep. This may never have happened before, or only rarely when you were very tired. But now it seems to happen every day. You try to think, and no thoughts come. You try to focus on God, or on

Jesus, and distractions flood your mind. You no longer feel that closeness to God, or to Jesus, that you used to feel. You are just numb. Your mind is sterile. You call out to God and you merely sense an echo. "Where are you, God?" you begin to ask. You feel as if God has abandoned you. Then you look inside yourself and wonder, "Am I bad? Have I done something terrible for God to abandon me like this? Maybe I am just not worthy of all these beautiful graces God has given me all these months. Maybe I have not been faithful enough."

Each day, you sit down to contemplate. And it is no different. Your prayer is so sterile, dry. You feel like one you love is no longer talking to you. You feel devastated. Then, eventually, after weeks of this dryness, you begin to feel that you are losing your faith. Since you no longer have the same feeling or interest in spiritual things, or even in the spiritual life, you can easily mistake this for loss of faith. Many people who have gone through this period of dryness stop going to church, and even stop praying altogether. Since it is no longer as easy to be holy and charitable and faithful in your religious practices as before, your old human weaknesses and failings begin to show again. You feel humbled and ashamed. You are just an ordinary sinful human being. You, who were just a short time before so holy. Now you are just like everybody else. You are no longer the holy person you used to be. In the darkness of your soul you cry out to God. But he still seems not to listen.

When a person experiences this spiritual dryness, which is called the dark night of the senses, it can be a great help to have a spiritual director, a priest or a person trained in spiritual direction who has an understanding of the spiritual and mystical life. Persons can be led astray during this frightening period. But it is essential that you go through it, because there are valuable lessons and graces for you as you are led gently by the hand of the Holy Spirit through this trying time. You learn humility. You realize you are no different, no better, no worse than anyone else. If God gives you grace, goodness is easy. If God does not give you grace, holiness is difficult, if not impossible. Before, you were buoyed up by tender feelings of intimacy with God. You were not living by faith. You were living by feeling, which is not very deep, nor does it make you strong. In fact, it gives you a false feeling of security, and a false sense of your own goodness.

Now that all is dark and frightening, and you no longer have those nice feelings, you cling to God purely on faith. You *are convinced by faith that* God is there. You *trust that* he has really not abandoned you. You do not feel it anymore, but you know it by faith, and even though you might be tempted to give up the spiritual life, and your daily contemplation, you still manage to persevere. You still struggle to do what is right, and to be caring and kind to others. You still try to be understanding and forgiving, even though it is so difficult, and you are not as successful at it as you were before.

The important thing to remember when going through this dark forest is that before you lived by feelings, but now you are living by faith. Your spiritual life is now becoming solid, and strong. You are no longer being good because you enjoy being good. You are now trying hard to be good, even though you do not enjoy it, but you want to be good so you can please God. You may not be as good at it, but your struggle makes you more pleasing to God than before when you were good because it was fun being good. You remain faithful to your time spent in contemplation because that is the time you have given to God each day. You remain faithful to it, even though you do not feel like it. You do it because you want to please him, because you want to be near him, even though you no longer feel his presence and his love.

The special thing about this phase of your spiritual life is that, although it is not pleasant and it is often downright miserable, you will learn more and grow more during this experience than during almost any other time in your life. And many of the things you learn do not seem to flow logically from your experiences. Random insights and solutions to problems just seem to come out of nowhere. It may be the way the Holy Spirit communicates with us when we open our souls to him. So do not make any radical changes or decisions while you are undergoing this painful trial. Just hold to the course. If you cannot pray, well, then, just sit there. God does not need your nice thoughts. In fact, he probably likes it more when we keep quiet, so he can share his thoughts with us. And that is the most important part of prayer. It is not what we can say to God that is important. We cannot tell him anything he does not already know. But God has many things to tell us. The problem is that we are too busy trying to tell him things, and have little or no time to be quiet and listen to him. So use this time of aridity to be quiet and just listen. You will be pleasantly surprised. God does speak to your soul during this painful time. He shares, very quietly, the secrets of his mind and his heart. He gives you rare insights into himself, into your own self, and into the hearts of others. It is very rewarding, even if not very consoling, because you feel so empty.

Hopefully, this period will not last too long. For some people it is short. For others it may last for months or even for years. I went through this horrible experience for almost eleven years. They were the most painful, depressed years of my life. I was only fifteen years old at the time when it started. It did not end until I was twenty-six. I used to sit in the darkness of the monastery chapel late at night and just to try to feel near God. I felt so lost. I knew I had to be faithful to my calling and not give up. I found a book on the spiritual life, and on mysticism, written by a priest named Tanquerey (not the same as the gin distiller!). I would devour that book in an attempt to understand what I was going through. It was a big help, and a comfort. At least it made me realize that God had not really abandoned me, but was just helping me to grow closer to him. But it was still painful.

Much later, when looking back on those long years, I began to understand that God was teaching me many important things during that painful period. I learned more about God, about myself, about people's struggles with faith and temptation and evil during those years than at any other time in my life. As painful as those years were, I gained valuable insights into the spiritual life, and about how God works in the souls of those who try to draw close to him. I do not think I could ever go through that experience again. I would not now have the stamina or the strength, but then, with the Holy Spirit's gentle guidance, I trudged through each dark and seemingly endless day. Today, I thank God for that time in my life, as I realize more fully how priceless were the spiritual treasures of those years.

Fourteen

"COME ASIDE AND REST WITH ME!"

One day, you will wake up and the sun will be shining, spiritually, and all the world will be bright again. God will call out to you, and you will rejoice that he is back, and has come to visit. After all that time of darkness, your soul will be flooded with light again.

But things are not the same. You no longer have those tender emotions you once had. They are gone forever. You are far past that. Your relationship with God is on a much more solid ground than mere emotions. It is similar to a couple who have been in love for many years. They no longer have those tender romantic feelings they once had when they were first married. They may not even have any of the giddy "in love" feelings they once had but they are willing to sacrifice anything for each other. That is real love. That is the kind of love you are now beginning to develop toward God. So do not be afraid. It is all part of the process of growing in the spiritual or mystical life with God.

Now, when you place yourself in God's presence and begin to meditate, you will notice something new. You will notice a new kind of emotion, not the kind you had before, but a kind of spiritual emotion. It is more like a joy in sensing a different kind of closeness to God. Earlier, you worked hard trying to understand and penetrate the passages of the Gospel stories you were meditating on. It was fruitful, but it was also hard work. Now when you meditate, thoughts and insights into the situation you are meditating on just flow freely; you are open to thoughts you may have never had before. They are beautiful thoughts, and they help you to understand difficult passages in the scriptures, and to find solutions to questions you may have been struggling with for a long time, but had never been able to solve.

You will also begin to notice that these insights and a new awareness of things occur not only when you are praying but at odd times during the day, at times when you might least expect it. It could be at a time when you are very upset with someone who has just hurt you deeply. While you are thinking of that person with anger in your heart, all of a sudden, you sense that that person has been undergoing some terrible private tragedy. You become confused and do not know what to feel. Then you find out that what you had sensed really did happen to that person, and you see why the person was acting so strangely toward you. The insight you had about that person makes you realize that God is helping you to understand his teaching on forgiveness, and how, if you want peace of mind, you have to learn to understand people's pain and misery, which often drives them to do things they ordinarily would not do.

I think my father had that kind of a relationship with God. Many years ago when I was teaching science, I brought home my Leitz microscope, which had high-resolution lenses. I invited my dad to examine the inner working of a plant cell. After watching the flow of cytoplasm and the movement of chloroplasts as they were manufacturing food, my father's only comment was, "That tiny cell is like a human being. No matter how insignificant a person may seem in the eyes of the world, in the eyes of God, that person's life is essential to God's work in the world."

Or, as one person said to me one day, "I had always thought that capital punishment is important to deter crime, until one night, when I had a dream. A man was sitting in the electric chair, waiting for me to pull the switch. To my shocking surprise, when I looked into his face, I did not see a criminal. I saw the face of Jesus Christ, and heard the words, 'Whatever you do to the least of my brothers and sisters, you do to me.' I woke up in a cold sweat, with my heart pounding in sheer terror. Since then I have always looked upon capital punishment as barbaric."

These are just a few examples of how God communicates with a person who remains faithful in a life of contemplative prayer. It is not make-believe. It is real. It is what Jesus promised to those who befriend him. As time goes on, the number and frequency of these supernatural lights increase, as your understanding of God and yourself and of everything in creation shifts to a much higher level. Life and people and issues are no longer black and white but many shades of color. You still see the backside of the tapestry, with all its tangled colored threads, but you also get brief glimpses of the beautiful pattern on the other side. Life inside your mind and your soul now is much more of an adventure than the life in the material world all around you. It is no longer boring or lonesome being by yourself. Spending time within has become an exciting adventure with God as your Companion.

But even this phase of the contemplative life is not the end of the adventure. The soul is not yet totally purified, and there is still more growth in this love affair with God.

This illuminating phase of your inner life with God may last for many months or years, as the Holy Spirit transforms your thoughts and attitudes to harmonize with Jesus' wisdom and understanding of human events and issues. That is the process of growing into Christ that Saint Paul was referring to when he remarked, "I live, now not I, but Christ lives in me." This is essential if we are to become authentically Christian. We have to have the vision of Jesus and the heart of Jesus, which is a lifetime process, since we are not born with God-like attitudes. God's thoughts are as high above our thoughts as the heavens are above the earth, as it says in scripture.

When a soul has passed through this phase of growth, the frequency of those remarkable insights and lights seems to diminish, and a new darkness sets in, the dark night of the soul that the great mystics speak of. This period is frightening for a timid soul, though if a person has reached this stage, he or she has been strengthened to endure almost anything, as the person's past life was not lived in a vacuum. Living life during all those previous experiences, and being faithful under trial and painful difficulties has steeled the soul for even greater tribulation, some of which will be just part of life itself, some part of the Holy Spirit's preparation for the next and most beautiful part of the mystical life, a union with God that is the closest experience on earth to heaven itself.

Saint Teresa of Ávila details in her autobiography the whole path through the mystical life, telling of some of the difficulties that a soul undergoes during this dark night. The only words that can adequately express what a soul feels are the words of Jesus himself on the cross, when he cried out, "My God, my God, why have you abandoned me?"

Deep down the soul knows that God did not abandon it, but the feeling of loss after many months of spiritual light and consolation of the previous phase is extremely painful and the feeling of loss of God's presence is similar to the death of a loved one. The grief is almost unbearable, but there is a purpose even for this, as the Holy Spirit prepares to deepen the faith and trust of this special soul who has given itself already so completely to the love of God. There is a painful depression, which is part of this sense of loss. Often there are other experiences that are an ordinary part of living, which may coincidentally happen at the same time. The person may lose family members or friends who are very dear, perhaps a mother or father. Occasionally, a loss of material possessions may take place, or poor health may set in. Although part of ordinary living, when these things happen at the same time as the spiritual feeling of loss of God's intimacy, the result is devastating. Where does one turn when even God seems far away, or no longer there? To get some idea of what takes place in this special soul, you might want to read the story of Job in the Hebrew Bible. The Book of Job describes in detail the anguish of a soul undergoing feelings of abandonment by God.

But, again, in the midst of the darkness, the Holy Spirit is developing an underlying strength and depth of faith that is truly extraordinary. The practice of heroic virtues flourishes; not just an ordinary practice of virtue but a stream of virtues in an extraordinary degree: patience, charity, compassion, prudence, justice, faith, hope, courage, perseverance. Along with these virtues a wisdom and insight into human nature is an appreciation of all that God has created, including God's tender love for humanity. We would all wish we could see God in the poor and the depraved. Persons who have attained this degree of holiness see God when they see the poor or the depraved. So it is not that they go through this darkness unprepared. Their whole past spiritual experience has been a preparation, much like the painful exercises of an athlete training daily for the Olympics.

In time, even this darkness passes. When it does, the joy and delight that awaits the person is beyond the ability of human words to describe. God now draws the soul into a relationship that is truly mystical and involves the deepest levels of the soul. It is beyond sense experience. It is even beyond the intellectual delights of the previous phase. In a very real way, the soul experiences an intimacy with God that mystical writers can only compare to a marriage relationship, a bonding of the soul to God. There is even a ceremony which takes place between the soul and God, which Saint Teresa of Ávila and Saint John of the Cross describe. Prayer has now reached a level of mystical contemplation of the Trinity and the role of each Person of the Trinity as it affects the Church and the lives of human beings. The whole purpose of God's involvement with the Church and with individuals is to mold in each the image of the Son of God. There is no other purpose to God's involvement in his creation. His interest is in us, his children, and in making us all beautiful masterpieces of his creation, replicas of his Son, who is the most perfect Image or Reflection of himself. The beautiful universe around us is his gift to us, a material symbol of his beauty, his grandeur, and his magnificence, for us to enjoy, and to remind us that one day we will live in his home, a place of glory and wonder far beyond the wonders of this universe and even our ability to imagine.

JOSEPH GIRZONE retired from the active priesthood in 1981 for health reasons, and embarked on a successful second career as a writer and international speaker. His bestselling titles include *Joshua*, which has been made into a major motion picture, *A Portrait of Jesus*, and *Never Alone*. In 1995, he established the Joshua Foundation, an organization dedicated to making Jesus better known throughout the world. He lives in Albany, New York.